After

and

Before

the

Lightning

Volume 28

SUN TRACKS

An American Indian Literary Series

SERIES EDITOR

Ofelia Zepeda

EDITORIAL COMMITTEE

Vine Deloria, Jr.

Larry Evers

Joy Harjo

N. Scott Momaday

Emory Sekaquaptewa

Leslie Marmon Silko

After

and

Before

the

Lightning

Simon J. Ortiz

The University of Arizona Press

Tucson and London

The University of Arizona Press
Copyright © 1994
Simon J. Ortiz

⊛ This book is printed on acid-free, archival-quality paper.
Manufactured in the United States of America.

99 98 97 96 95 94   6 5 4 3 2 1

Library of Congress Cataloging-in-Publication Data
Ortiz, Simon J., 1941–
After and before the lightning / Simon J. Ortiz.
p.   cm. — (Sun tracks ; v. 28)
ISBN 0-8165-1423-2 (alk. paper). —
ISBN 0-8165-1448-8 (pbk. : alk. paper)
I. Title.   II. Series.
PS501.S85   vol.28
[PS3565.R77]   94-5761
813'.54—dc20   CIP

British Library Cataloguing-in-Publication Data
A catalogue record for this book is available from the
British Library.

Grateful acknowledgment is made to the following
publications where some poems in this volume first
appeared: *West Wind Review, Writers' Forum, Wambli Ho,*
and *Smart Magazine.*

Contents

2 Common Trials: Every Day

4 Near and Evident Signs of Spring

Preface

Winter is legendary in the Dakotas, as everyone who has
ever lived there or has heard about it knows. When I lived
on the Rosebud Sioux Indian Reservation one winter sea-
son, it was not only a storied time to be remembered and
talked about later on but a real and very present fact. Snowy
frozen days, bitter cold nights, and endless wind. The South
Dakota winter was forever—at least it felt like that, snowy
wind and blizzards and blistering cold from November
through mid-April. Just like any legend, just like any story.
But this was more than legend or story. This was a reality
that could not be denied.

I've felt I have never been very good at facing reality
nor at dealing with it. And when I lived in South Dakota,
working among the Lakota people, teaching at Sinte Gleska
College on the Rosebud during that season—"after the
last thunder and lightning and before the first thunder
and lightning"—I needed a way to deal with the reality of
my life and the reality in which I lived. The winter prairie
surrounded me totally; it was absolutely present in every
moment. I could not put on enough warm clothing nor
be prepared enough nor was there a way to avoid it. The
reality of a South Dakota winter demanded to be dealt with.
So I was compelled to write the poetry in *After and Before
the Lightning*.

On a daily basis and in a moment-to-moment way, I
found this poetry reconnecting my life to all Existence with

a sense of wonder and awe. Every line and word, every image and thought, every sensation and emotion was an explicit item and notation about what was happening in my life that winter on the South Dakota prairie.

The narrow asphalt strip of Highway 18 from Mission to Okreek is not actually very far in distance, no more than eighteen miles, but across the prairie hills late at night under a starless sky or in February during a storm piling deep snowdrifts across the road, it feels endless. It feels like somewhere between South Dakota and "there" because it feels like traveling on the farthest reaches of the galactic universe. The day sky, the night sky, the planets and stars, the constellations of the Milky Way, the vast and boundless cosmos of Existence—all these were vividly present, immediate, and foremost as context on the prairie.

When the poems came about and I wrote them, I felt like I was putting together a map of where I was in the cosmos. I'm not certain that "map" is the correct term, and I'm not certain if, as a writer and poet, I was even successful in noting and expressing what I wanted and needed most of all: reassurance that by facing reality—winter and my life— I was doing the right thing. Yet I believe now I'm doing the right thing and I will stand by that.

Recently, someone asked me about my use of the subjective personal pronoun "we" and the objective universal "we" in the poetry and prose-poetry passages. In some instances, my references were to an actual person, who was immediately present with me, and in other instances I was making general, omniscient references. Perception and expression of emotion and imagination, telling dreams and plans, sharing direct experience and personal history, relating real and actual events, at moments in the mixed contexts of memory, speculation, fantasy, and intellectual thought are all of a process. As author, the writer is within this process in both the subjective and objective "we."

Why do I use galaxy, horizon, moon, stars, universe, lightyears in the poems? Why do I speak of traveling across vast spaces of prairie and time? Why do I choose the ideas of destiny and memory, and what do I mean by them? Why do I relate such abstract images and ideas to the immediate and material facts of the winter prairie that was the present and elemental environment around Mission, Okreek, Rosebud in South Dakota? In composing a map, the only way I could do so was to locate myself in relation to the endless snowy sweep of the prairie with its low rolling hills, the sparse stands of trees along frozen prairie creeks, and the distant blue horizon merging into gray-white sky. Time and place and memory. The prairie hills and blowing snow and distant ranch houses and ghost buffalo. This was the evidence of Existence. This reality was there, and I was there within it. Every moment, every act of my being was defined by the reality I had to acknowledge. Not to acknowledge this would be to deny Existence.

When a friend read a version of *After and Before the Lightning* some time ago, she referred to it in terms of the darker moments of my life. She said it dwelled upon desperation, death, and loss of hope, and I could not disagree at the time she said it. As an Acoma Indian in the Americas, the dreaded reality of despair, death, and loss because of oppressive colonialism has been too often present, and I cannot deny that. No one can, certainly no one who understands and has undergone debilitating colonization. My personal experience and history have been burdened with too much of that.

Yet, like facing the reality of upper-Midwest winter weather, which can be fifty degrees below zero and more on the way, it's possible to know that burden as more than just desperate and difficult and impossible to deal with. Indian people, especially the Lakota of South Dakota whose homeland has been the prairie for generations and generations, know the harshness of this reality. And yet more than any other knowledge they have, they know the sacred beauty of the prairie homeland which they regard with wonder and awe.

Living and writing evolve as I continue to live and write. I am most conscious of my life as a journey, and what I write is a map that comes about every moment for me. Every day is like that and that's my certainty, a memory of how my journey has been till now.

Simon J. Ortiz

They say the time of cold and snow is the time
for stories. And, yes I'm sure, it must be true
for poetry too. It has to be true. It has to be.

These poems come from a winter I lived on the prairie
of the Rosebud Indian Reservation, working with Lakota friends
who are the grandmothers and grandfathers, mothers and fathers,
daughters and sons, sisters and brothers of their people.
They are the true caretakers of their beautiful prairie land.
Always among each other and with the land, they are relations.

For all my relations.

Lightning I

This evening we are not eager
to approach Okreek. The close hills
above the little Lakota village
are tenuous with black forces.
Electricity as mere physical notion
can never be measured or held
by mere bone, blood, imagination.
It takes more than nerve to see
what creation wreaks at once.
Opening prayers of humility
cannot ever bear the total shudder
and crackle of one's only life
settling into molecules, then atoms
fusing apart, becoming life again.
The safety of Okreek is assumed
only. It is not affirmed fact.

Lightning II

Safety is not the destination reached
when we drive into Okreek, home
only yards away. There is a steel fence,
and the dragonlight dances furiously
from prairie hill to hill. Shadows tumbling
down all over, lightning bursting on its mane,
the mind is a panicked horse.

So we stop, turn off the car engine,
study the rusty gate for a long moment,
knowing only imagination is not full knowledge.
What happens in the act of millions of volts
of fiery electricity meeting hair, bone, skin?
The question peers through the cold rain.

Mere distance from the storm isn't anything.
We wait for the wind and rain to pass,
hoping for miracles we've heard about.
Life can be a laughing matter, we know that,
but even that knowledge is not much comfort.
The moments of our exuberant arrogance
are not useful right now. So we wait, measuring
the fact that storms don't always last long.

It doesn't last long, we find out. It passes.
Though afraid, I still get out of the car.
Taking one more breath, I walk up to the gate,
tap the rusty gate like it was a manta ray,
jump back, wait for the dragon to crackle alive.
Nothing happens. I feel the cold tap of rain
on my face and shoulders. Nothing happens.
This time I pray: Safe passage for you, dragon,
sacred mysterious one, and safety for us again.

The
Landscape:
Prairie,
Time,
and
Galaxy

1

Hot coffee at Ron's is always good. Black, strong. Laughter,
stories, friends. Ron looking somewhere else, deep inside,
or far away as usual. Up there, all around, with the stars, or
within. The cosmos.

David slams the door, walks in, sheds his coat and gloves,
takes off his snowboots, and stomps into the bathroom. Ron
says, "You folks don't come here for coffee. You come here
to use my bathroom!" Yes, our laughter.

Earth Mother, She Cares

The tenth November day now
of snow which doesn't melt,
just evaporates mostly.
And ceaseless, dry prairie wind.

Volcano thunderous in Columbia.

It may be ten and ten
more days of snow and wind.

Freezing. Thundering.

We can do nothing else
but pray, pray hard.
The earth mother cares.
She loves us, and her blood
boils, her bones shiver.

Just pray hard, pray hard.

Snow drives across the road,
and we have no power.
We're standing still,
and it's the snowy wind
and the prairie that move.

It may be ten and ten
more days of the volcano.

Pray hard, pray hard: hard.

3

One morning, one winter he got up. According to his role and responsibility as Kuutse-hanoh Naishdeeyah, he'd go in the early morning to pray at one of the sacred places. As Antelope Father-Elder, he'd go in one of the four directions. "Haaweh-shthih Shiwana, I'll sing you a song, I who is the Antelope Elder," he said. And he sang for the Snow Shiwana, the spirits of winter. His song was: Hahdhi-shra Haaweh-shthih Shiwana? Hahdhi-shra Haaweh-shthih Shiwana?"

All around in all the directions were thick snow clouds, and on the stony ground was deep snow. It covered up the trail and the water holes on the mesa. He sang: "Where are you, Snow Shiwana? Where are you, Snow Shiwana?"

Well, later on, telling about that morning, he would say, "As I was singing to all the directions, looking all around at the Haaweh-shthih clouds, suddenly I fell into one of those frozen water holes covered over with snow!"

" 'Right here I am, the Shiwana,' the Shiwana said to me. 'Now, you've found me.' "

And we laugh, because it's good to laugh with story, because it's good to laugh with memory. This story remembers him, amoo-uh my father. Beloved my father.

Driving, the Snowy Wind

Tried to get to Rosebud
at noon yesterday.
Failed.
Drove back from Mission
to Okreek.
Because I forgot my briefcase.
The snowy wind.

Returned from work
in the late afternoon.

Prairie hills quivering.
The snowy wind.

The snowy wind is fierce,
insistent, unrelenting,
picking up dry snow
off the hills, turning the hills
into churning clouds and the sky,
blending everything
into one cold surging,
exhaling, forceful breath.
For long seconds, driving
into the breath is blind.
I have to make my song durable:
Sing for the snowy wind,
the breathing power of the prairie.
Sing again for the snowy wind,
the breathing of the prairie.

The far hills are no longer far hills. The horizon has merged
into the galaxy. There is no end to things. It is all one, one
distance, one dimension. Together in a fabric of winter, sky
and land are sewn together, and the rivers and creeks of this
prairie are arteries and veins of one body. And we, atoms
and cells, move with the sinew of wind, frozen grass, ice-
laden trees, the poor clothes we wear, and the weak car we
drive. We are graced with a winter certitude we can only
acknowledge and cannot deny.

South and West

A diesel truck roars past us
right at the top of a hill.
I see the driver take one look.
I see him swing his heavy hands.
The murderous wheels spin viciously.
        Nothing
but the powerful sweep of the oily wind.

Not even a shadow,
only a cold dread left behind.
If he is lucky enough or dangerous enough
on this icy road south and west,
a man will get to North Platte tonight
and Denver early in the morning.
Forgiving, the prairie hills guide him
into the white, blue-ing distance.

Morning, the Horizon

There were pheasants
by the plum thickets
and in the pine trees out front.
Brilliant birds, vital
upon the snow this morning.

Later, east of Carter,
we travel on the horizon.
We are finally the blue horizon
of this high prairie.
We've become the distance.

We cannot be anywhere but here.
How we see is from within.
We have not traveled very far.
It's always the same distance.

I shall wait for tomorrow morning
eagerly, the vital brilliance.
And the blue horizon we will become.

Meaning

The low sun's light is a flat blade
on the black highway.
Nothing can measure distance here.
I look, there are only the rolling hills.
Nothing is behind.

The cattle are gone,
driven somewhere else, closer to barns.
Days ago when the wind was blowing hard,
there were horses standing in a hollow
near the highway, huddled by a haystack.
Like a second skin, there was snow
on their haunches, on their backs.
With no need for semantic sense, the meaning
of winter is this fact of nature—
a simple dimension of the frigid knife
under the stirless evening sky now.

When we return to Okreek, the little Lakota village secure in the prairie hills from where we left this morning, I look at the small stack of wood on the back porch. It's covered by the snow that does not melt, only evaporates. It doesn't always have to be so hard. Pray hard then, pray hard, and tell stories. The stars are not so far away.

Vital Margins

Bitter cold margins of wind flowing
from hill to hill.
                         Snow rivers, sinuous
veins of vital organs.
                              Story,
though it's still of the bitter cold, helps.
"Steel plate in his head from the Marines
in Korea," Seth says. "When he came home,
he had spells. One night, winter and cold,
he left to go to the outside toilet, you know.
Somebody found him, thirty miles away, cold,
no coat, nothing, thirty below degrees,
almost gone."

The courage it takes is sometimes marginal.
Yet our lives are durable, as tough

as sinewy wind, up then down, love and hope
more vital than anything else.

Story helps. We live the margins we've seen.

The Edge Facing Us

The snow has blown
under the garage door
and carpets the cement floor.
The yard light silvers the snow.
It is so quiet and shadowy dark.
Far from anywhere but the prairie hills.

We know the stars are reliable.
The moon is not forever
but, too, we know it returns.

What we trust is the edge we offer,
a universal plane, the side
that is the symbol of our existence.
Our breath, skin, eyesight.
The quiet night's cold face
shows us its edge too.
It is the silver snow.

NOVEMBER 20

I've forgotten part of the story, but I remember she said, "The
girl and the other children were standing at the door, their
hands held out, ice in their hair." She spoke in the voice of
her mother. "Her husband, my father, said, 'Close the door.
It's just the Indians. They are used to the cold.'" She spoke in
the voice of her father, the voice she heard her mother speak.

When the woman looked at her husband, he was glaring
at her. All around them, the walls were solid with winter.
Silently, the children of the frozen woods stood there, ice in
their hair. Would they always be there? And the woman, her

husband, their daughter, their future? And again the children with ice clinging to their black hair, would they always be there?

"This is the quilt made from that story," she said.

Salvation

Jim Bob, the rancher on the hill
above us, works in the dark cold
between his garage and barn.
His truck engine races fiercely.
His tractor tires churn the snow.

Salvation, I think, is his brutal winter work.

One morning, I saw him by his house.
He was a dark stature against the sky.
I waved at him, and he waved back.
I'd written late into the night before,
and I'd risen early again to write.

All day long, he had worked the day before
until long hours past his suppertime.
In vain, the winter work finally isn't done.

Brutally driven, I think, is not our salvation.

An Insistent Gentle Animal

The winter wind pushes upon the walls.
It's a roar that uproots trees
and yet is so gentle to the hills.
The prairie is an enormous surging animal
I saw the other morning near Assman's Tractors.
In constant shivering motion,
its massive loins more than half-dragon,
more than half-snake, it was a spirit-creature
from our other galaxy.

The galaxy is within us,

ferociously powerful and dangerous
yet so gentle always we trust it
like we trust a kitten.

                              The wind is gentle
with this creature, and we have to be gentle too.
Ever so insistent and bold and loving,
it brushes upon the walls
we don't trust ourselves without.

I wake up to a cold house. The walls are hard, dense, stony solid, and outside the icy walls are fiercely struck with sunlight. Stepping outside, I can't help but shiver. Snowy hills are bright; the sky is far. Winter is not yet here, but I can feel its daring youth and unwithering pride. It's as hardy as this morning is.

I decide to get wood. Jim Bob has told us the wood down by the creek is already spoken for. Friends of his. I decide we need wood. If his friends want it, they have to get it quick. Otherwise, I get it. Snow is more than ankle deep. Prepare myself mentally. Not much to it: just be cold enough, kind of angry, no words, decisive. Doing it is to do it. Put last of the wood in the fire and there's no more. And I know there is wood down there, by the creek. Dead trees, dead branches.

The decision to do things requires no more than what is necessary. Food, shelter, clothes, heat, safety. The moments may be unclear of how it will work out, but immediacy is the main power. Just do it. Simplistic perhaps, but what else can there be? Our decisions are relatively simple once they become necessary.

Bits of the sky, tiny shreds it has become, fall once in a while. Not snow but the sky torn by the cold and wind. The huge presence that is more than half-dragon, more than half-snake shrugs, its sinews laborious but not urgent. The decision to get wood is part of that. I say, Winter Spirit, breathe us into you, hold out your hard hand in which there is strength and shelter, let us be a part of your stony skin. And I sing too. Pray.

Later, with the fire roaring hotly, wild flames and dragon children flare up in the belly of the stove. The grain in the dry oak is thrilled. At the edge of my heart's membrane, little creatures dance. There is warmth and a harking back to memory, to the child at the horizon when the earth was born. Tiny dragons and flames wild-dancing, singing, whirring like many-colored doves they become and become.

Hearts and Hearts

Blue jays and pheasants outdoors,
and we are indoors.
How we are to each other
is within our ken.
They see us peering
out of the window.
We see them in the yard.
Each of our lives a distance,
yet together in this season.

When I go into the deep cold
of the garage, I hear the flutter
of sparrows between the roof
and the ceiling.

Each of us is an adjustment
to the force that nature is.
Feathers, skins,
hearts and hearts,
eyes that meet
for seconds, instances holding
to the fragile margin, the season
we come to know as our bond.

A blue jay pecks into the hard crusty snow. Working for its food, driven for food, busy by necessity. The pheasants, the same, edge out of the creekside woods into the clearing in front of the house. They poke their beaks at something dark upon the snow.

Yesterday, we talked about commodity food. Indians, poor people, need to eat. You have to eat. Rations, welfare, no choice. You have to work, I said, if you can. Work your fingers to the bone—what do you get?—like the song says. Bony fingers. You have to laugh. My mother, my father always afraid of welfare, the government, the law, the state, and so they worked hard and borrowed against payday which sometimes didn't come. Scrabbled. To be free, to stay free, to know the dignity and integrity, the value of life and heritage. I remember seeing a newspaper article my mother had on a kitchen windowsill, an item on welfare. That's all, no other memory of it except the feeling and cold and hunger of that time. I was a teenager. You have to work.

When you're cold, hungry, when you need things, you do what you can, yes, do what you can. Sometimes you do even the necessary thing you don't want to do: go to the government office, stand in line, wait your turn, cry inside, tighten your face, wait, be insulted, pretend it doesn't matter, pretend it's not that cold and you're not that hungry.

Watching the blue jay and pheasants, I think of my parents so fierce with their courage and determination to be free. Watching the blue jay and pheasants, I think too of how people are driven to slavery in today's world.

Comprehending

Sawing firewood, I feel my skin,
blood, muscle working
to warm the cold air. My mind
comprehends the possibility

of the final margin.
There is a tight pain
at the junction of my left shoulder,
and my neck leans away from it.
Even in pain, I yearn
for the overwhelming awe I feel
which links me to this day,
the trees, birds, snow,
the gray-blue light of the prairie.
The rancher, Jim Bob, drives
by in his tractor, hauling hay
from the hill to the corral
where his cattle bawl.
Swirling around, they are hungry,
urgent yet patient, following
the tractor closely.
When Jim Bob backs up and stops,
they approach eagerly.
This is winter and its patience
trying us, needing to know
that we will endure.
The saw needs my agility,
my tired shoulders.
There have been moments
when I've had no reserves,
when I've run empty,
and the horizon was only an ache.
It is the comprehension
of this margin that awes.

Destined

Snow flies furiously eastward
and prairie hills hunker down.
The walls, windows, and roof
shake and shudder.
Everything feels destined.
Yesterday afternoon,

men came with a truck.
They were heavily dressed.
They loaded some cattle.
Their work was methodical and accomplished.
How far, I thought, is it to Sioux Falls?
How far, I thought, is it to Lincoln?
Destiny is not a distance.
Bitter cold and endless,
it is this South Dakota wind and snow,
a destiny we cannot deny.

Morning: Dawnlight holds steady, and silence does not betray the winter shadows. No echo therefore, not even a shimmer. Loss is never known. It's simply a fact of winter silence.

I do not open the curtains: Let the little warmth stay for a while. Let the cold wait for a while.

I start to build the morning fire.

Dream: Quiet Wind

As the fire starts,
I remember the dream.
It is a quiet wind,
an old barn at the foot
of prairie hills.
No one is there,
no cattle wandering around.
Old loose boards settling
into place, never doing so
in any final way.
A Norwegian farmer
and his son built it.
How do I know that?
Not from experience,

not from memory.
Yet, something took place,
something had happened.
Just like the barn was built
by a man from Norway,
the next generation
with him loyally.

The crusty snow does not give
up its grains easily to the wind.
A thin mist fills the air.
These prairie hills hold dreams;
they have these and more.
The horizon is their essence,
and it offers us this morning.

Morning radio: The weather report says, "Freezing rain, no
driving recommended." Here, the weather in winter is always
"news," whether it is good or bad.

Between South Dakota and There

There isn't a single car or truck
on Highway 18 from Mission to Okreek tonight.
Except for us.
                    There is nothing but the night sky.
Stars.
        The moon a huge pendant.
Stars somewhere
                between South Dakota
                        and somewhere
there in the cosmos.

Where we go is always down this road,
believing the prairie gives way to machines.
Yet because our belief is weak,
we look to other notations.

                                    The far signals
from the prairie hills and the sky above
and all around.

                        It is a mirror; we could be the image.
Travelers on silver roads between galaxies.

It is cold though for travelers.
The heater fan doesn't work.
Our fingers and toes tingle.
Yet we are hardy, enduring, patient.
We are anxious to pass through this galaxy to the next.
Traveling in the night sky,
                        believing we are its image,
we know we will reach there.

As we come this night from the western hills above Okreek,
the sea is there before us. The lights of this little Indian village
are a seaport town waiting for its fathers, sons, husbands to
reach the safe shore.

Voyage to Haven

Safe haven
in this dark night,
the swells of the galactic seas
bearing us toward unseen stars farther
away than we thought. Knowing we can never again
calculate the wind and the distance
we longed for, we still know
the certain gauge of hope.
Now we come to this,
the dark haven.

Knowing

It felt like that.
Bearing from the west on Highway 18,

we angle slightly south, downward, gliding
from the prairie hills.
                              Here
ghost buffalo dream, huffing at the crust of snow,
the grass beneath. It is the sea out there though,
the silent cold shore hugging the little seaport
of Okreek to its threatened shore.
                              The fog is dense,
merging with the unseen dark sea.
It could be that way, who knows it can't be.

We are at times far from shore.
We hunger and yearn for the welcoming lights
of little villages where warmth waits,
and mothers, children, wives scurry to check
the boiling soup.
                    It felt like that,
even as we know it can't be, knowing it could be.

There is always the moment of silence. No motion. Just the
quiet held breath. Exhaled light. Breath of light. This cold bril-
liance the prairie hills give forth. God's sky eye. Oneness a
circle. Within this, the silence.

Field of Scars

Old scar tissue does not heal
as readily as scar-free tissue.
Scars upon scars. Indian lives
are like that. Breaks
upon breaks.
                    Skin, hearts, bones.
We endure nevertheless.
We thrive nevertheless.
Though we can never be innocent again,
we have to always hold true

17

to the course set by vision
beyond ours.
It is the galactic ken
that is the sacred bond
that must not break.
It would be sacrilege,
so even on the scars we hold
and build, cherishing the flesh beneath.
This is the field that is our earth.
It is from here our seeds grow.

Thanksgiving Day: Going to get wood in the cold garage, I say a quick prayer. "Thank you, Creator Spirit in the trees, in the snowy prairie hills, in today's cloudless sky, in all the little items of life, and in all the large things. These things are ourselves. Thank you for us every day, every moment, in all beginnings and endings."

Thank you even for the televised parades from New York City and Philadelphia.

On This Day

The electronic mechanics and wizardry
of tv connect us to Detroit, Philadelphia,
New York City, bouncing us from planet
to planet swimming somewhere beyond us
and returning us to this little village.

How we fend for ourselves is beyond us
anymore, yet somehow we manage to trust
ourselves still with a need that is beyond
the wizards of computers and corporations.
This is the need we must always struggle
to keep, knowing our hunger, so our anger
will not always be bitter, instead knowing love
is what will keep us returning here
from beyond, always returning here.

Just at this moment, the sun and a small breeze decide to let a bit of snow fall from a poplar branch. Gently, it drifts down, alights on the snowy ground. The bit of snow agreed and decided also. And the sky beyond the trees, the prairie hills, and my eyes. In this one moment, one event, all these things, all these are one.

Thanking the Pheasant Hens

Five pheasant hens
cross the road in front of me
just over the hill east of Carter.
Quick sudden turn to the left,
and in the rearview mirror
I watch a car behind me also swerve.

Somehow, we're mindful of things.
Sorghum stubble fields snowed over,
scattered distant farmhouses,
wobble in the car wheel.
All these, staiidzee. I thank
the pheasant hens for bringing me
to notice. Staiidzee, all these.

Later on, I will remember the good smell of bread, fresh-baked, as I walked into the house. Several loaves sitting on the kitchen table. Two pies in the oven, a warm fire. "I was tired from driving. Sometimes the prairie highway got to me." The long and cold prairie road, the horizon so far away it felt like a dream you can't remember and you try to but can't. "I walked in . . . and there is nothing like the smell of good fresh bread."

Stories are as basic as good bread and a warm fire, no more than that. Stories that make the frozen icy roads bearable. Yes, they say winter is the time for stories. No other time, other times you work. Now, it's cold outside, so you sit indoors, stay warm, and tell stories. Eh heh, that's what you say to show that you're listening, that you're not asleep. So gather the children around, roast piñons, get out some salted parched corn.

"Let's see, I don't remember that one. . . . Howchaatya, it's too cold, but not as cold as 1954. And not as cold as 1938. I remember. We had our cattle up the canyon toward Tsuu-schcki Tsaigaiyamihshru. Why is it called that? Well, you know, it's because of Tsuuschcki. That Coyote, you know how Coyote is. He was on his way to Zuni to get married that day. . . ."

They say that, that winter is the time.

"In those days, people would go on top of Horace Mesa to gather piñon nuts. Once, in October, they went for two days. On the second day it started to snow. It snowed all afternoon and into the night. . . ." No, it's not that way. The story goes its own way. In my mind, the words go their way, follow-ing the basic story plus the imagination and memory, plus the way I have experienced things. It is how the story goes, my mother's and father's words, their experiences in my mind, and my mind's own knowledge.

Imagination is a harking back to the source but it is also more than source.

"They gathered dyaiyaahnih for two days, and then an old man said, 'We better start homeward. It's going to snow very heavily.' So the people packed up and drove their wagons and horses down from Horace Mesa. And just as they turned onto the road toward their home, my father—your grand-father—looked northward where they had been. And there were thick clouds above Horace Mesa, and it was snowing, just like the old man said it would."

Snow that October, the language of experience, sensation, history, imagination are all in the story and how it carries forth. Story has its own life, its very own, and we are the voice carried with it.

Long Roads

The long roads from here
into the blue snow distance.
Cosmic lines drawn forth,
arcing whispers, junctures
of the prairie hills,
shadows and the moon facing us.

We are certain of destiny,
having never forsaken it,
and we have all the time
in the world.
Already, we have intersected
the space encircling us.
Long roads are our history.
And the dream's songs
are imbedded in blood-memory.

Across the Prairie Hills

Distance, destiny, memory
across the landscape.
Across time and galaxy.
My father described the haitsee.
It is a thin oak limb,
bent and tied into a circle.
Intersected by cotton string,
the string making four points
on the circle and at the center.
North, West, South, East, Center.
Sacred places and directions.
The four sections of the circle
painted yellow, blue, red, white.
It's a map of the sky-universe,
my father said. You make one
when you prepare to travel.

So you will always know
where you are, to where to return.
Haitsee, a map of the universe.
Knowing the distance
is always vast, realizing
destiny is somewhere beyond,
we need memory to know our way.
Here across the snowy prairie hills,
we need this, the truest road.

Juncture

As I straighten up
from building the fire,
I feel the pain at the juncture
of my back and hip.
The sudden notice of it
makes me twist my shoulders
and back to locate it.
It's right there.
Maybe it's the way I stooped
to get wood from the garage,
movement without balance,
the cold, a number of things.
It's okay, I say to myself,
noticing it is enough,
it'll work itself away.
It's not enough, my bones
and muscles say.
My mind wants to agree.
The sudden lurches
in my history catch me up sometimes
I know, and it's this pain
that is the juncture this morning.

What I Would Want

Ryan tells of two boys
lost this snowy, cold afternoon.
"I went looking for a big buck
and ended up looking for lost kids.
Their father was back at their truck
freaked out. His boys
just had on thin jackets."
It wasn't very cold this afternoon
but it grew dark very quickly
as the snow started falling again.
I can imagine the father's fear.
The anxiety that sits like a bird
back in the winter shadows.
You could fly away, like the bird,
a stark portent upon the bleak afternoon,
but it would be in the wrong direction.

The boys were found though.
Ryan is tired, cold, and groggy.
I would not want to test this prairie's mercy,
and if I did I would want that bird
of anxiety to be the hawk
that survives these winter hills.

Crossing

Go to the post office in Mission
in the morning before the storm hits.
That's what the weather report says,
something from Texas, something
from Canada. And we're in the middle.
All the way, the highway is slickery.
We're full of tension, quiet, expectant.
Trust the road we travel, I pray.
Expect that what we traverse is fragile.
We have to accept our quavering frailty.

Later at home, fix turkey soup.
Cut leftovers, onion, broccoli stems.
Add couple handsful of noodles. Wait.
Put wood into the stove in living room.
Look outside, intermittent snow falling.

Friends to come later in the afternoon.
Will cut the small roast, serve vegetables.
All these things, the warm walls, soup,
small necessary comforts on this day.

We expect we will quaver some days,
traveling on bad roads, even at home
fixing dinner. But we know, too, the traverse
cannot fail us crossing the storm's middle.

Friends write me from Arizona, Colorado, New York, from
the West and East. From here, where the storms from the
Panhandle and the Canadian prairie meet and clash, I wish
them well. I hope they sit gladly in warm living rooms. I hope
they fix vegetables, leftover turkey, noodles into good soup.
We need those things, especially in the middle of busy storms
we raise up ourselves. They wish me well. I send them good
warm smells from this kitchen, fragrant smoke from the heat-
ing stove, my breath given out to all the directions, and a
twinge of this wintry prairie cold.

Blind Curse

You could drive blind
for those two seconds
and they would be forever.
I think that as a diesel truck
passes us eight miles east of Mission.
Churning through the storm, heedless
of the hill sliding away.
There isn't much use to curse but I do.
Words fly away, tumbling invisibly

toward the unseen point where
the prairie and sky meet.
The road is like that in those seconds,
nothing but the blind white side
of creation.
                      You're there somewhere,
a tiny struggling cell.
You just might be significant
but you might not be anything.
Forever is a space of split time
from which to recover after the mass passes.
My curse flies out there somewhere,
and then I send my prayer into the wake
of the diesel truck headed for Sioux Falls
one hundred and eighty miles through the storm.

Icicles fascinate me. Their appearance, their formation, their
disappearance. Something in the process, the innate cer-
tainty of nature we finally have to accept. Fluid become solid,
crystals suddenly though gradually formed, locked. Motion
of water stopped. What we know is meager. Awesome, in-
comprehensible order of the universe in the prism of an icicle
clinging to the roof edge. Held for the instant, my fascination
is locked into an icicle.

Foolish Believers

This is the inexorable, momentous fact:
process.
                      We are only a part of its moment.

Yet there are corporate laboratories
where methodical work goes on
day and night, men and women laboring
to create—

yet only succeeding
in putting to death process.
Laboratories and machines
do not heed the essential nature
of process: motion and change.
Men and women want to halt it
and start it again by their will.
And they do from time to time.
They stop the inexorable motion
for hesitant, feeble moments,
                              exalting,
never quite knowing what they have done.

It is foolish to believe we have the power
to lock process into a crystal or cube.
For when we believe it is our will,
we do not see icicles forming
and we will never be enough awed.

Claiming Territory

It is a magnificent idea. Claiming territory.
Just climb the next hill, cross the river,
and say, "This is mine." Nothing
scurries, nothing shifts, the Creator says
nothing.
                    It is simply spoken,
                    simply carried out.

                              This prairie
is full of snow now, when months ago
it was grassy green. It is all spacious unending,
a beautiful heartland of continual motion,
continual creation.

                    The seas of millions of years,
glaciers, huge ferns, then buffalo, then the people
of this prairie, then now.

                              Such things,
such life, such change. And then one day,

one of them, a stranger, said, "This is mine."

                                  The river
gathering waters from the north, moving southward
in an earth-nourishing flow said nothing.
The sacred horizon hills didn't budge. Yet everything,
everything was awed, dismayed, dazed
by the incomprehensible idea.

                          This is mine.

To See the Prairie Sun

Almost mid-morning
and the sun is so low
in the trees, I have
to bend down to see it.

Clear path through snowdrift.
Work is work, hard: puff
and unbend once in a while.
Arm muscles stiffen quicker
in the cold. Think: blood-
motion-veins-arteries-heart.
Fingertips tingle, blood
eagerly answering thoughts.

"The moon, the stars,"
friends shout the other night
close to midnight
as they were leaving,
pointing upward.
Beyond and within this daylight,
the stars dispersed become
one light of this bright morning.

Soon the sun will reach
its southernmost point.
Kuuwahmih-shooqku. Tihdyahmih
stih dzunehgkuuh. Northward then
it will travel, days growing long.

Right now though, as I shovel,
the sun is so low
I have to bend down to see it.

Coping

Paroxysm of bitter cold wind
though we know it's been coming.
Unprepared as ever, we never
quite get it, how we must cope.
Last night, the wind rattling
the windows, trying to lift
the roof, and this morning is
a deeply throated frozen moan.

The radio report of downtown Winner at 10 degrees above
and a wind chill factor of 30 below, wind blowing 25 mph
doesn't mean anything. Gales of icy mist tumble about us,
bending us. Yesterday, we got news of the fierce storms of
Great Falls, Montana, and Keokuk, Iowa.

This morning is fact, not radio and tv news. Okreek, at the
edge of which we sit, is a little Lakota village lost somewhere
beyond the horizon of the prairie hills. It will never be a news
item on radio and tv, but we know the sheer cold fact of it
now.

Sun Prayer

Look, the sun!
For some brief moments,
masses of clouds permit light.
An odd patch of torn silvery orange cloth.
Pray for light then, always
the need, these moments.
Sun needs prayer.

To Here, We Return

This prairie could lose us.
The horizon is lost
in the icy sunlight glistening
off snowfields.
                    The sheer plane
of memory and the last hill are lost
behind us. Only the necessary,
the most immediate is with us.
We cannot be anywhere but here.
Led by these South Dakota winter hills,
we are destined to turn again later,
when we have to and shall return.

Windtrails carved in snowbanks. Snowbanks sculpted like
no one else's fingertips. Snowtracks contoured into forms
of music no one else's but ours. Sheer memory is not much
use, it almost feels like. For the moment, it is only the nec-
essary that is important. And we cannot be anywhere else.
Perhaps at the point of death, it's like that, nothing else but
the immediate knowledge of life, no memory of the past, no
foretelling of the future.

Prairie sunlit sheen hurts the eyes. You have to feel the pain,
the consciousness of light interacting with nerves in the eyes.
Where are the hills, the horizon we have always known as
reference? Following shimmering icy light, there is only a
plane of undulating surface leading outward to where the
horizon should be. We should stop but motion is urgent in us
always. We can only allow destiny to turn us later, to return
us, and we have to let it. We can only return to this snowy
prairie, and it can only return to us.

Common Trials: Every Day

2

Barren

Last night's wind
has blown some snow away.
Prairie hills
are hints of yellow-brown.
Brittle, dry grass
pokes through the surface.
A skinny horse by the road
scrapes for something below.

This land is barren, poor.
The people just as poor.
I ask a foolish question,
halting on the possibility.
"How . . . can? Can they . . . ?
the people get back . . .
their lives?"

Answers falter.

How our lives turn, bending and breaking sometimes, and then healing, and we're not always sure. Several nights ago at the beginning of another storm, I listened to us talking. Stoking the fire once in a while, smoking cigarettes. Ed tells the story of a man who came to a house, hungry, tired, and he was turned away. And then a hungry dog came to the house, and it was turned away. And then a man who was a king and a god came, and he was treated royally and generously. And to the astonishment of the people of the house, he explained the visitations of the hungry and tired man and the dog.

I tell about Aliyosho, the young boy, and his brothers, and their mother. A poor family. They had heard about a reward to be given by the rey, the king, and the older boys, who were brutes and insensitive, told their mother to pack them a lunch. They were going for the reward, to win the reward. Aliyosho, the young boy, wanted to go, he begged his mother, and she told him he was too young, only a child. But finally she gave her blessings and let him go.

On his way to the rey's house far to the south, Aliyosho met an old horse that was sick and dying which the older boys had ignored and neglected and insulted. And Aliyosho gave the old horse water to drink and washed its hot painful sores. And later, Aliyosho, the humble boy, after many hardships and tests of his courage, endurance, and patience won the reward given by the rey.

The older boys? I don't know. They probably told their mother some kind of made-up story.

Later that night, Ed's voice changes, and he says, "We all make mistakes." He doesn't explain but I feel it, and I understand. It's true, the bending and breaking, the mistakes. And then the healing. Sometimes it takes years. Sometimes like the people who turned away the hungry man and the hungry dog, we don't see God. We don't see the poor, and we don't feed them. And sometimes, the poor are ourselves. Years it takes.

Storm

A young Indian in Sioux Falls
was forced to bargain
himself for years into state prison.
Another just got thirty years.
Two more wait to be tried, facing life.
Or death.

> All these years
> we've been bargained.
> Fifteen, thirty, life years.
> Death.

Let your shoulders sag, breathe deeply.
For a moment, the storm has abated.

A warm spell began yesterday,
temperatures reaching the low thirties.

Only man's rage continues to storm.

Inter-Crossings

Thirty or so deer
on the north side of the road
between the Witten turnoff
and Carter's Store.
On the south-facing slope
of a hill gently falling
into a little valley.
Above the deer, miles away,
is pink-tinted rising land.
The last orange glare
of this winter day's sun.
We ride for the horizon on the west,
leaving the prairie darkness in the east.
This day, the deer, hills, the valley,
the turnoff, evening sun,
these are what we know
of such inter-crossings.

The deer are beautiful, unafraid, coming slowly down the hill,
browsing in the frozen grass and snow, some raising their
splendid heads. Picture postcard, that's what it looks like. The
deer ignore Highway 18 traffic crossing the Rosebud toward
the prairie beyond. Dark brown with white tails, stark pres-
ence upon the white hills. This prairie is theirs. We have to
keep knowing that.

Without fear for the moment, they've come out of the
curving dark line of oak thicket in the ravine west of them.
Dyaanih Kquuyaitih, this song is praying for you. Too quickly,
we pass them by on the other side of the fence. Like it was
only a dream, only a pretty postcard. But no, it is real as any
inter-crossing.

Watching the Ice

We pick up White Horse again.
This time he's headed the other way.
Standing by a stalled car,
he waves to us.
It's me again, he says, laughs softly.
Where you going? I ask him.
Has a small can, car's out of gas.
We drop him off at Carter's Store.
Watch the ice, I say.
Okay, he says. You too.
                              Waves, balancing himself.
We wave, balancing ourselves.

DECEMBER 5

Notion of Time

The sun is on the southern horizon
as we're driving back from Mission.
Pink-tinged snowscape, a subtlest notion
on the horizon, something far away

moving toward us.

                    Kuuwahmih-shooqku,
the southernmost point the sun reaches.
And then it turns northward,
its journey to make the days longer.
It has nothing to do with time
but simply an awareness of motion,
the circular path of the earth
around the sun, and the sun moving
in its own path through space.
                            Turning northward,
we don't know time. Instead,
we are time, the subtlest notion of it
that is the horizon moving into us.

The Vision of Finework

The road on the hills above Okreek
cuts through snowbanks five feet high.
Strata of snow, layers in a finework
only the wind has the skill to do.
What the mind is capable of is not much,
only a certain kind of arrogance,
other than that not much for survival.
The snowbanks have no idea of our coming
nor of our leaving. It doesn't matter.
But there is something there unnoticed,
willing to be like the wind has left it.
It is this that saves us, the finework
that is our salvation, our poetry, image
that gathers our vision into a skill.
It is the wind's work over many nights,
and it is the force of our ignorance
which allows us to leave it alone.
This finework, layered snow, always lasts,
always capable of not much more than that.

Nothing To Do With Halley

We are ice and stone,
fire and air,
                comets in the galaxy.
The tail that glistens
in our wake is our own origin.
The moment of creation is each day.
                There is no wonder
about our curiosity
of what is in the heavens.
It is ourselves we try to see.
The stars, planets, moons, comets
are our beings, we are the reflection,
and they are ours, no more, no less.
Halley has nothing to do with it.
The comet can only be known
by all of us coming into being.

On late-night television, two U.S. scientists talk about why the U.S., Russia, Japan, and several European nations have sent up satellite probes to photograph Halley's Comet, pass through its tail, see it up close. The scientists both agree it is "for the tremendous prestige" that would accrue to the nation to actually get there, to acquire information, and be the first to answer the unknown. That's all. One of the scientists says, "It costs as much as one B-1 bomber." Prestige, national standing, power. That's all.

In one of my short stories, an elder who's a grandfather asks, "And then will they know?"

The Possibility

The old man could have told them.
His grandson explained to him what was happening.
"See those astronauts, Grandpa," he said,
pointing to the tv screen. "They're on the moon
to find out what's up there, to find the origin
of life, where and how things all began."
The old man couldn't believe it,
and he couldn't believe his grandson talking,
talking like the scientists who didn't know.
He thought about stone, water, fire, and air.
And he had to believe it was possible—some men
didn't know or had forgotten

> stone
> water
> fire
> air.

He couldn't believe it, but it was possible.

Coming from Valentine, Nebraska, crossing the state line into South Dakota, the long distance dark of the great prairie is unfathomable. Nothing is known beyond the limited scope of the car headlights, beyond the curve. I think we don't survive by instinct much at times. We survive and go beyond by the constructions made by our hope. And history, experience, identity. Memory is our experience at the same time memory is our hope. We can't see the horizon, yet we know it's there. It has to be there since we do have some rough estimate of it. We know enough of history and experience to know it has been there. Our identity is founded on it; it could not possibly not be there if we want it to be. The future is secured without the construction of certainty. The only way we know Mission is on the horizon we yearn for and finally Okreek is because we want to get there. We would be false to ourselves if we did not believe that. There would be only the gloomy dark, a winter that has entered the spirit. Do not go gently, Dylan Thomas whispered loudly into the dark.

Enormous Knowledge

It is amazing
how much knowledge
we have of hope.

Whisper bravely
into the dark,
Heart,
        whisper loudly.

Tonight, a man in a green coat and a gorilla mask held up a supermarket in Sioux Falls, South Dakota. Even before Christmas, in fact three weeks before Christmas, folks go crazy.

Destination: Destiny

On the way to Rosebud this afternoon,
there are people walking along the highway.
One footstep after another, hoping for distance,
a necessary place that is destination.
Time not much to do with getting there,
we know what it's like leaving things behind,
hoping to reach the source of our destiny.

On the way back from Rosebud in the evening,
day falling quickly, others are still walking.
Having never gotten there, we return back
on a familiar road, our destination always.

Time, in fact, has to do with everything.
We hope nothing has remained the same.
We still hope for a destiny that's been reliable

till now.

It couldn't have been more than fifteen minutes later. He looked again at the clock radio below the tv. It was 7:30 P.M. The last time he checked it was 7:15. Damn, he thought. He laid his magazine aside and got up again to look outside. The snow was still coming down. The light from the bedroom lit up the flakes falling into the azalea bush, the leafless azalea bush. The snow kept falling, and he stood only for a moment at the window. A man in a green suit, no, a green coat and a gorilla mask, had held up a market downtown in Sioux Falls. Damn, he whispered. A gorilla mask, green suit coat. Damn.

He had gotten out of bed finally, long after she had left that morning. Bam, the door had slammed. Just bam, that's the goddamn all. And he had washed the dishes, vacuumed the floor, even fed her dog, stared at the phone, made the bed. Bam, the sound caroomed in his mind still, after all day long. A man in a gorilla mask and wearing a green suit. That's how he would say it when she drove into the driveway. No, when she got out of the car and she was coming in the door and he was opening it. He would smile broadly and say, Honey, a man in a gorilla suit and a green coat held up a grocery store in downtown Sioux Falls. Tonight, can you believe it? And he imagined he would laugh, and she would too. Would she? No, she wouldn't. Before she left, she said, I wish you were dead. I hope you're dead when I get back, if I get back. And bam, the door went. Damn fool, he said. Green coat and a gorilla mask. Only a damn bam fool.

DECEMBER 8

Lakota people here keep asking me, "Well, how do you like the weather?" I grin and say, "Well, if it would get seventy degrees I would like it fine." We laugh. Outdoors, snow is piled high and roads are frozen solid. Actually, the sun broke through for several days and today the clouds are scattered. Some roads are thawed and safer, but the piles of snow will last till March I'm told.

The other day at Antelope Cafe, White Hat said, "Don't talk to me about the snow is beautiful. When ranchers and cow-boys have to get out there in the snow with the cows, it's not very beautiful." We laugh too.

When I ask Agnes in Rosebud when the next snow is going to come, she looks out the window at the sunny snowfields and says, "I know an old woman who said to me she didn't know where she was getting some wood." She pointed at a small closet. "Look. I've only got that, a handful of sticks." We don't laugh.

This prairie and more prairie of snow stretches for miles be-yond miles, so vast it's no use to estimate it. You just have to let it be, just like how you are at this present time in your life. You have to let it have its own time and presence.

41

Here and Now

The thermometer outside the window
reads twenty degrees. No wind here.
Ponderosa pine looks frozen stiff,
icy needles motionless.

Everything has stopped.
Imprints of my footsteps
in the backyard go nowhere.

It is simple enough
permitting silence, a clear act
of being nothing more than now, this moment.

The pine, my footprints, the chilled air,
they don't stir. They agree for the moment.

Leave things alone, I tell myself. Leave them well enough
alone. Good advice, but I step out back and study the sky
above and beyond the bare-limbed elms, oaks, and ash. My
mind doesn't tell me anything but my bones and skin know
the insinuation. They've been animal too long, their gathered
spirit can tell what's in store. Instinct garnered from the touch
of ice granules and glaciers slowly lunging toward us; it
knows more than mere intellect can ever know. When my
fingertips touch the cement slab at my feet, my bone and skin
urge themselves toward caves not forgotten, and when they
feel the snow yet to come out of the vague distance beyond
the hills, I go back indoors. Leave things alone sometimes, I
tell myself. Close the door gently.

Searching

In a patch of brown weeds
bent westward for the rest of the season,
a pheasant wanders and pecks about.

Like the old veteran I watched one winter.
From the third floor window of Ward 8
at the VA hospital, I would see him.
He would go toward the river,
enter among the winter willows and reeds,
become a shadowed bird, searching
for what I didn't know.
                                        The bird now
leaves the patch of dead weeds
and still eager for something
crosses the road below the hilltop house.

Part of the day spent wrapping Christmas gifts makes me sad, lonely, even fretful. I've always been too full of myself, I know that. Remorse is too much when it's a signature. I've gone home from school, work, Army, marriage, VA hospital, divorce, jail, from wherever, bearing gifts. Although sometimes not, when I've had nothing but my bare life. I've not been the prodigal son entirely but there's been that feeling, and so I've carried gifts home for the holidays. This year I'm sending them, and the remorse I've relied on too many times, almost seeing it as a friend at moments, is not welcome.

I cut the wrapping paper, fold boxes, sign name tags, write loving notes. The small gifts for my children will get there, and they'll be welcomed. There is no use to fight remorse so rigidly, so strongly, but there is no use in giving it much credit for anything either, however. At the end of the day when I'm finished wrapping gifts I am tired, my back muscles tight and painful from sitting on the floor. I've welcomed this work, having decided this is what I must do, and I am grateful my remorse has not been so overly urgent as I begin to fix supper.

What We Come to Know

When I begin to cook
venison Ken and Betty
brought over the other night,
I think of the food it is.
And I think of the Deer it is.
Its odor is raw and dark,
even as it is cooking.
It's not been since high school
I've hunted and shot deer.
There hasn't been much
I've done about it,
the fear of guns, explosions,
wounds, and blood. Death.
I feel uneasy when I see Deer now,
understand their furtive stance,
watch their eyes, prepare
to flee, to hide if I have to.
But I do cook the wild meat,
thankful for the living flesh
Deer is and for the generosity
of friends and that helps me.
I will probably taste the fear
of guns and explosions
in the wild flesh always.
And I will probably always
study their eyes and prepare too.
But I think of what Deer is
and what friends are
and what we come to know.

Haaweh Song

So the Haaweh softly comes,
gently and deliberately.
Here I am, the Shiwana
of the prairie sings,

where I've always been.
Smiles, certain of care
and love and needed water
it brings to all things.
Chuckles, always mindful
of growing and changing.
The Haaweh comes softly so.

It wasn't my father who told me the story of the morning the
Haaweh-shthih Shiwana found him by dunking him into the
icy pool of water. It was my mother as she fixed breakfast at
home in McCartys, in New Mexico. Her voice soft, deliberate
in her movements about her small kitchen, mindfully laughing
at the memory of her husband, my father. "He came home
and told me what happened to him," she said. Memory is
more than story; it is symbol and gift. When we sat down
to eat, I caught my mother's eyesight lingering upon a pile
of stone my father had brought down from the mesa north
of Tsuuschcki Tsaigaiyamihshru to build an addition to their
house. Gentle, white snowflakes tumbled down softly upon
the sandstone, becoming the memory that is more than story.

Freedom From Scavenging

"Did you get anything from scavenging?"

"Nope. Freedom is too important."

The struggle not to have to scavenge
is too strong an urge still.
The struggle for knowledge
is too strong an urge still.
The struggle for freedom
is too strong an urge still.
The struggle not to have to scavenge
just to be able to survive,
that is too strong an urge.

Journeying

A night's hard journey
without stars
is taken in any case.
Homing on moments before,
we do not lose our way.
We are always there. Within.
A circle of night mirrored
by a circle of day.
Our journey is not fearful
as we accept each homing star.

Journeying back to Okreek
through a sparkling, million-eyed universe,
the road is a constellation known
only within the knowledge that is ours.
Who else would travel across lightyears
this night just to feel its worth?
We know more than we're sure of,
and we don't skip any galaxies.

Origins

Three pheasant cocks
and two hens
under the pine tree.
Sleek and fat,
they look prosperous.
I think of their origins.
We're told they're from China.
Now, it doesn't matter,
they've grown well here.
Fat and sleek, rare
for this lean prairie.
They're gorgeously plumed,
strutting quite regally.
And I, an Acoma son
transplanted here also,
hungry this morning,

look closely at them,
considering origins
and what we're told.

Forever

At Deetseyaamah, I liked looking south
at the mesa above "the white bridge"
that was always about to fall down
when I was a boy but it never did.
In March, snow was still on the mesa
even when it had melted everywhere else
since the snow was on the north slope.
I don't know, I just liked looking at it
because I could see stones and junipers
and snow always there like forever.
Of course, snow lasted for only a while
but that was enough, enough to stay
in my mind forever, like it is right now.

Look right now. It is a view of snow.

DECEMBER 11

Yesterday, the few sunny days were gone, gone suddenly
back to blowing snow and chilling wind. It was back to fight-
ing for balance again. Frozen rutted paths seemed more
slippery and dangerous, and I felt tentative and impatient. I
was running from the Science Center at the College to the
Lakota Studies trailer. Albert had just gotten out of his car,
and he saw me. He took off his glove and held out his hand
to me. Smiling a big smile, a big Lakota man offering a big
hand. I could be crawling on ice floes, slipping away from my
life, nothing but swirling icy black below, and he offers his
hand. He doesn't say anything, and I don't say anything. For
a moment, there is nothing to say. His hand is the solid, safe
prairie land, warm and welcoming, and I cling to it for dear
life.

Beauty Unmatched

Icy bits of snow skittering
is a sign of the tilting planet
as we drive back from Winner.
The hills are a fluorescent blue.
Nothing can match this beauty.
It is ours now, the pink evening
lunging gently toward us, the sky
mantled all around. It is ours.
Let the planet fly, we would cling
without a word, knowing mystery
is definite in our dreaming ken,
our stories and songs heard widely
as anything that holy ever was.
Beauty without question, unable
to be described, simply accepted
for what it is as skittering snow,
blue prairie, and a pink lunging sky.

We lunge toward it, driving a little compact car, such a poor
excuse for transport. But then, what else can it be? Horses
would not dare the wind at this hour, a sailboat would floun-
der on the shadowy hills, and dragons are lost without imagi-
nation. For now, what there is is apparent, this evening's
dimension carries us forward. The little American-made trap
that is this car does dare more than it can handle. Our dreams
are fortunate and forgiven. Where else can we go but into
the dusk descending quickly all about? Horses, sailboats,
dragons leap bravely into the wind, skirting the hills, and we
do not falter nor flinch as we are all heart and spirit in our
lunging toward the falling light.

Storming Toward a Precipice

A diesel freight truck
roars toward us.
A precipice is no mirage
for its metal plunge.
It is headlong nevertheless.
"It carries its own storm,"
I say dryly, feeling
my tongue wet my lips.
Trapped steel storming,
the faint line just so,
                    just inches
                    just split time,
                    just nothing more
than luck keeps us alive.
The mirage of metal storming
is a precipice, no mirage.

Survival in the Cold Dark

9 P.M. Jim Bob and his wife
are out in the dark by their barns.
Cold necessary work, a steady struggle
to go on, to shelter their cattle, to survive.
Blizzards are predicted for tonight
just as they've always been.
                              Steady
                              and brutal
                              and final.
And as always, the man and his wife
lurch without question, without qualm,
with shoulders hunched against the pain
in the dark, knowing the desperate
noise quivering from within, the need
for sheltering for which we wail.
I know the steady struggle of work
just to survive and I know

it's possible to survive predictions,
but unlike Jim Bob and his wife
I don't think I will ever accept
the steady and brutal and final act
of hunching into the cold dark.

I don't know though. I may say that I won't, that I can't. It's too brutal I may think, too desperate a way to live. But it's living nonetheless, living in the eye of the predicted storm. You can't just give up, you can't always expect that it will pass you by. You can't always be behind doors closed to the blizzard. You just can't be immune to everything going crazy around you.

Still, it is too brutal a way to make a living, ranching on the South Dakota prairie in winter. But the cattle bawl, and I admit my heart is breaking. So I tell myself, This is a way of life for them, it's necessary. But it's dropping toward zero and by morning it'll be forty below.

Ranchers have to make a living even when a living means selling your cattle for a price below what you got for them last year and the year before that. And your fingers numbing even through two layers of gloves. I may think and say it's too brutal to live that way, but I know too that Jim Bob's and his wife's children have their eyes pressed to the windows, peering out toward the barns, their noses growing cold. And no matter what, and without question or qualm, I would plunge out into the dark cold dropping toward fifty below. I would know that Christmas is only fourteen days away. I would know.

Respect and Recognition

Morning fire flares easily,
no hesitation or wavering.

Flames from paper catch
to oak bark, then to wood.
It should always be so easy.
But it's not, that's for sure.
The cold is dropping lower
and the wind has blown snow
against the windows
and across the roads. . . .

                              The mind
is drudgery, more weight than usual
at times, and we don't know
how to leap like fire catching
easy some mornings.

                    That's okay though,
the respect and usual recognition
of the cold and the snow
becomes our certain survival.
Without this, we would be the fire
that is hesitant, wavering.
We would not know continuance.

Choosing words is a waste of time. Let the words choose
you, let them choose their own place, time, identity, mean-
ing. Writing is a waste of time in a sense because we try "to
fit" words into an order that makes sense to us and to other
people. That's arrogance, ego, artistic illusion. No matter
what we do, what we think and feel, what we want words
to do for us, we can't fit them into an order that's ours. They
have their own power, their own magic, wonder, brilliance.
Where and how they fit, that has nothing to do with us. The
only thing we can do is recognize, admit, and accept that. Let
words choose us. Let language empower us, give us beauty
and awe. We cannot do anything about it. When we think
we can, when we choose words, it is a waste of time.

Beauty All Around: Borrowed From Dinéh

Now the sun is so low on the horizon.
Now there is a rainbow circled all around the sun.
Now there are three suns, one is in the center.
Now there is beauty all around.

The song-prayer must be for this.

Looking eastward, just above the hills at mid-morning,
circle around the center sun is immense, shimmering
in rainbow colors, the circle complete,
its bottom arc at our feet, and standing before it
we are within the sphere.

> In beauty before me.
> In beauty above me.
> In beauty below me.
> In beauty all around me.

Nothing but the totality of the sun
and winter snow and being alive and knowing
it could be nothing more than beauty.

This is the song and the prayer.

DECEMBER 13

First Prayers

First, say a prayer.
First, put on the coffee.
First, build the fire.
First, get dressed.
First, say a prayer again.
First, these things.

It's strangely quiet, perhaps only because storms have been
predicted for the past two days, and it's unusually not cold as
we have expected. The prairie sun is shining, trees bathed in

strong yellow light. The rancher and his wife have been fran-
tically preparing for the storm the past two nights, working
late, and their cattle have been bawling. The mind has pre-
pared for it too, looking out for its body, to see how much
clothing it has, that there's enough wood, and hoping. But
it's quiet, the wind that was strong yesterday though not
fierce must have suddenly changed, turned toward Minnesota
or Iowa, or just dissipated. The quiet is a bit unsettling, but
the prayer is for thankfulness, praise for the sun, goodluck to
the wind, reprieve for us.

What It Takes

At 10:10 P.M.,
it's 22 below in Pierre
and 20 below in Valentine.
North and south.
Which way is the wind blowing?
To the southwest.
Good, maybe it'll miss us.
To the northeast.
Good, maybe it'll miss us.
Actually, we'd be right
in the center where they'll meet.
And Jim Bob is still out there
putting hay out for his cattle.
The faith, hope, and belief
it takes at 10:10 P.M.
with the skies so clear
you can feel the stars
right at the tip of your fingers,
feel the cold tingling brilliance.

The newspaper cites a tragedy, what could it be called but
that, this is America right in the midst of its self-made turmoil,
anguish, loss, what could it be called but tragedy.

The Farmer and the Banker

What happens when faith breaks?
When hope whimpers away?
When dark belief becomes a question without relief?

So it's a farmer in Hills, Iowa, no longer able to prove
he can get up at five o'clock in the frigid dawn,
night not over at all.

So it's his despair finally wringing his wearied hands
at last in finality.
So it's his shotgun no longer useful for anything
   but brute desire.
So it's his debt to earn a living for something,
   for someone, for anything
and everything and nothing that answers fatally.

A banker is dead.
Another farmer is lost to wrath.
And wives merely left to loss.
That's it.

Ringing pellets absolute in their trajectory,
terror at last settled, the debt unpaid as planned,
the question unanswered.

Ann's mother tells a story of her mother and aunt sent into
the Missouri breaks with nothing but a knife and some string
to learn how to survive because their father had no son to
teach how to survive. "Can you just imagine?" she says,
astonished.

DECEMBER 14

Driving back from Winner last night, there was an unusual
light in the low clouds to the west beyond the hills above
Okreek. Mission, we thought. Rosebud. No, the small Lakota
town's not big enough to throw light onto the prairie clouds.

It was past eleven o'clock and too late for the dusklight hours before. We didn't know what it was. Perhaps it was a signal from a galaxy beyond.

Maybe Rapid City almost one hundred and seventy miles west or Valentine thirty miles southwest, we thought. The road, Highway 18, snakes all over the prairie, generally going west and east over and across the hills and sometimes you can't exactly tell when it's slightly turning north and slightly turning south. Turning to look for the winter stars, we did not see any. Only the light which was vaguely layered. It could be anything, small prairie towns giving off homing lights, the far sunset on the Pacific coast, the shimmering margin of the horizon unseen in the dark vast night.

We left it alone, the mysterious source not tugging urgently. And as we turned off Highway 18 into the little village of Okreek, I took one last look. It was there above the road climbing the prairie hills, right there toward the next galaxy.

Silence. Quiet.

> Sparrows
> skittering noisily
> from the leafless elms
> into dry reeds.
> Sudden silence.
> Quiet river frozen
> in a sweep across the grayness.
> Above, solid, immobile.
> Thin clouds, distance
> not real, only certain.
> Forever.

I make phone calls today from here to the West. Distance is not vast or limitless but it's more than desired. There is no acceptance of the separation between things. There is too much that has to be mended. Phone calls are no more than wire and voices trembling across the prairie, bounding off the farther mountains, whispering above the blue snow that's too silent. Yet, that is all we have to share with these moments. The vast and limitless are within the necessary knowledge we have.

Buffalo

Dawn

Coming

We don't know what to do sometimes. Even with the dearest of friends, we mess up. They invite us to lunch, and we don't go. We make some kind of excuse or no excuse at all. It's impossible it seems to explain what it is that throttles us, leaves us without compassion. We don't understand, they don't understand. So we leave things up to chance, to question and bafflement, hardly forgive ourselves, don't really deal with anything, leave our friends worried about our health, our sanity. It's a kind of security, the ambiguity.

A Story of Courage

By the highway out of Mission, going south
about five prairie miles, a rusty green tractor sits.
Behind it on a low hill a quarter mile away
sits an abandoned house with broken walls,
no windows, no doors. Everything's been over
for years.

                 When was it the farmer quit?
Just quit one hot August afternoon, no rain
for five years, eyes itchy from sweat, hope
all lost, bills unpaid. It wasn't a question
of when or how come, it just came to that.
The tractor too old, engine long dying,
front wheels thick in useless dust, the sun
blazing fiercely unjust. And he said, Okay.

Now, the hills all around are stark with ice,
the years still too long, the sun merciless
sometimes even in January never mind August.
We don't know our own power to forgive.
We don't really admit the land is stubborn
and brutal at times but never in a final way.
And, bereft of forgiveness, we don't know
why we say, Okay, as if everything's over.

On that highway south of Mission a few miles,
we cannot fail that farmer's last promise.

Okay, let's say, this is his courageous story.

Savage and Animal Yearning

Already there is more light in the morning.
The savage in me renews his faith again.
The animal in me remembers each new day.
Nights and days remain cold, but Sun
is powered by new prayer and it knows
for what we seek and for what we yearn.

Perception of change in the season's weather is definite. The savage and animal know the long and many years. There is no ambiguity in the light through the trees. The horizon hills are not hiding anything. To and from Okreek, the roads are still slippery and dangerous, but the sun pours its light onto the prairie and the prairie receives gladly. We know our faith works. With prayer, the human in us must be patient. Always there is more to come, and we will accept what comes.

Vengeance, the violent repeat of murder and suicide, is reported in the news. It's not "news," having nothing to do with local, state, national, or international news, but more like prophecy. These are the acts of bewildered dreamers dismayed by the American Dream, and finally they have come to know illusion and the lie.

Never Fulfilled

The skill it must take
to let go fatally without anxiety holding
back. A moral thirst unquenched.

Yet still being true to self
in an oddly peaceful way.
                                    When it comes
to this who but the last surviving child
will know what it was that took
the finger beyond the river which no longer
could ever soothe.
                              South Dakota was that moment
yesterday. Eternity made no sense,
only justified in the glaze
of two men unable to see anything
beyond. Stricken.
                              Their wives and children
unable to choose. No one knew what happened.

Redemption Slipping Away

This is mid-America, a dream
of hollow gold, a dream
of rich illusion, a dream
of embellishment, a dream
of fancy. A dream.
                              This is the dream
that has returned. This is the dream.

Listen to them,
the sheriffs, senators, ministers,
psychologists, good neighbors.
Listen to them,
the seekers, the desperate, the hungry, the dreamers.
These are the ones holding fast to the dream
even as they feel the illusion slipping away
until no forgiveness will be their redemption.

It's not that strange because we have become so used to
deeds that make no sense. Two men killed their wives and
children and then themselves. They lived not far from each

other, but they didn't know one another and yet they had so much in common. How this society-nation must thrive in order to avenge itself, that's the odd belief, a strange code. It has sent its soldiers and merchants and bankers and engineers all over the world, and they have returned. They've come back hoarding riches, and they've come back senseless. The strain of duty must have a fierce and murderous vengeance which now wreaks havoc upon the fringe that has worked to hold sanity together. Now nothing is sure, not even the strangeness of becoming used to senseless deeds. But in that is a measure of our salvation.

To Be

The sun blazes fiercely at midday
but heatless.
Fireless, it is
               that way we must blaze.
Ferocious with necessity,
urgent to thrive each day, each moment.
Time and place sacred, the endeavor
to become and be.

           Being is not more
           than being,
           the necessary fire
and light, even without heat as known.
Our heat each stroke
of our breathing, sacredness
necessary to acknowledge
for it all to be whole.

A gentle winter wind moves bare poplar branches slowly back and forth against the blue icy sky. Nothing more than that. Clouds far beyond the trees at the horizon. What distance shows us is a closeness of vision. We are never far from the horizon but within it, the circle of sky. This morning the snow melts even without heat. The sun exalts light and energy received by crystals of ice. "Being" is necessary to know in a sacred way. We grasp it every second, every instant of awareness, and we <u>must</u> be aware. Without willingness to be aware, there is no light. We are within the sacred moment of awareness when there is light. To be is the willingness to be, nothing more, nothing less.

To Gather Them With Love

Just over the prairie hills
men and women murder each other.
Crying, we don't hear.
Knowing, we don't know.
Hiding from each other
is the dearest sentiment we have.
For we cannot bear the crying,
the knowing, the fearing.
We must reach our sight and love
over the fearful hills
and gather those murdered women
and men back into the sacred life.

JANUARY 14

Dawn

The sun on the prairie horizon
throws light
halfway up the trees
by the creek.
             Merely that:
my perception simply
acknowledging its context.
Morning, winter, sky
all around, a bird chirp
in the garage eaves.
A small prayer then: Thanks.

Nothing more,
spirit-mind-heart-presence
all we need, the dawn
on the prairie is ours.
And we, the dawn's own.

Walking toward Winner yesterday, trying to hitch a ride, I
looked all around me. The silent, long prairie was all around
me. I chanted something like this: long silence, longer than
long silences, longer than lost echoes, the horizon is mine,
ours, the echo is ours, the silence so long the echo is long and
becomes silence.

The sun in the southeast was so low, barely above the crests
of prairie hills. So low you have to bend down to see it, I
thought. That's the way it was on the prairie road. I wondered
how it would be to sleep by choice somewhere out there in
deeply frozen winter. I wondered how it would be to sleep
not by choice but because somehow for some crazy reason
you got stuck. It wouldn't do to sleep then. Just wouldn't do.
The long silence would be a long sleep, longer than anything
else, I thought.

Becoming Human

We are given permission
by the responsibility we accept
and carry out. Nothing more,
nothing less.

People are not born.
They are made when they become
human beings within ritual,
tradition, purpose, responsibility.

Therefore, as humans, this we do:
Sun Father begins red

in the east.
Stand and be humble.
Red through trees,
moments changing each instant
into the next change,
each change tied to the next.
To be human is to have
a sense of being with self.

Sun. Red. Trees.
Our hearts' eyes seeing
inward and outward, accepting:
Stand and be humble.

The more names you have the more of a person you become.
That's what I've heard. I was telling Tom that yesterday after-
noon. Values, education, social change, cultural corruption,
what is and what isn't. I have to dispute him at moments. I
tell him, The knowledge we derive from the education we get
is our own. Knowledge is determined by our cultural, spiri-
tual, linguistic, political environment. The knowledge from
the community and context here cannot be anything but the
people's own. This is not Chicago, St. Louis, Dallas, or Rapid
City. This is Rosebud, the Lakota homeland.

Our names are both Indian and American. We have so many
names now we don't know them all. In a sense, we have
become more of a people than ever before.

Our Names

Our names are our struggles.
Our names are our victories.
Our names are our places.
Our names are our journeys.
Our names are our circumstances.
Our names are our stories.
Our names are our lessons.

Our names are happy times.
Our names are sad times.
Our names are strong.
Our names are our own.

Albert was telling about when he was a boy. He and other boys would go along the prairie creekbeds in winter. The creeks were frozen over long periods of time, and the ice would be buckled up. Sometimes crawling, the boys would go through the tunnels under the snow made by the ice lifted up from the creek. I could see him then, a Lakota boy. When he got older he said he worked for ranchers around here, around Rosebud. He became a cowboy, he was a Lakota cowboy. Now, Albert's a teacher. He's taught at the college for several years and other places. He's older now, and, needless to say, he is Lakota still and always will be.

After reading several Alice Walker poems this morning, a terrible feeling starts shouting in me: I'm tired of carrying your dead around. Bones and shadows. Nothing but bones and shadows. Carry your own dead.

What Is a Poem?

Picture a man going from place
to place, finding a bone here,
a skull there, a chunk of stone,
a shard of plate, an old calendar,
a rusty bolt, a piece of cloth.
What is a poem but that.
What is a poem but that?

Four sparrows hop about in the backyard
near the path to the trashbarrel.

They pick scraps and bits off the ice.
Two blue jays come upon them,
and the sparrows don't hesitate to flee.
> What is a poem but that?
> What is a poem but that.

The man sees a murder one morning.
This is in America.
Another day he sits in a government office.
This is the place it happens.
Things happen. Murder
and waiting in government offices.
> This is not a poem.
> This is not a poem?

That man cannot be saved.
Everything must be saved before he will be.
He doesn't eat for days.
There is nothing to eat.
> This is not a poem?
> This is not a poem.

What is a poem? This is not a poem.
This is not a poem? What is a poem.
What is a poem but that?
What is a poem but that.

JANUARY 20

The Dreamer's Song

Yes, the morning sun.
Yes, the land all around.
Yes, the people with us.
Yes, the dreaming dream.

With song, the blood runs strong.
With song, the eyes see clear.
With song, the heart is full.
With song, the spirit does dream.

For we cannot be denied.
For we will not be held down.
For we shall not turn away.
For we must not quiet the dream.

The dream is the sun and the people.
The dream is the song and the spirit.
The dream is always "we are everyone."
The dream is always the dreamer.

Happy birthday, Martin Luther King, Jr.!

This morning I'm glad about television because on the Morning Show or Today Show or something like that, people are talking about Dr. Martin Luther King, Jr. The dream and the dreamer. Yes, the dream did not die; it will never die. It is the way blood flows. If it flows into the dreadful streets, the sun will shine on it. Bright sun, bright blood! And someone will see it, and he will step into the street. His own blood flowing, flooding through him. The blood of history flowing like a river. The river will not stop. The dream will not stop. It cannot. The blood of the dreamer will keep flowing, flowing like a river. So I'm glad and thankful for tv this morning.

Ironic it is that television was the huge and powerful media force that made Martin Luther King, Jr., so much a part of our lives. The marches and demonstrations in the South, the speeches in Washington, D.C., news conferences, even his murder in Memphis, all that. And Dr. King, magnificent, heroic, personable, passionate, his words and image hopeful, inspiring, and comforting in the struggle. Impossible dreams articulated by a man who spoke of what people dreamed about. Television, even with and in spite of all its deadly and deathly indoctrination and commercialism, ironically made it possible for people to dream impossibly of freedom too.

Early, the Prairie Awakens Me

In the quiet cold dark
this morning,
the wind is pushing
at the frail walls.
It's already gained entrance,
I'm just awakening to it.
                              Early

this morning, hours
before anything else,
it wove its way
into my bones and muscle,
hid itself into my mind.
What saves me afterall,
again, is I have to let it.
It chooses where to go.
Like ours, its endeavor
is to face each dawn,
weaving through walls
and tree branches, following
snowy trails, leaving
its tracks upon the prairie.

It saves me, once knowing
I have to let wind do its work,
waking me in the dark,
hoping on it, accepting
its cold shudder afterall again.

This morning the sun will be late. It will take its time. Light,
light, we are hungry for it. Already my skin, my eyes and heart
are lurching away from shadows still heavy. It will take time
for light to come. I know there are men and women who are
cold, trembling, not knowing if light will come again. Perhaps
they have given up waiting. Some mornings they have waited
hopelessly, finally hopelessly, but then it came against all the
odds they had placed. They had blasphemed as I have, having

lost all belief in hope, but they have finally smiled, accepting
they are to know the light afterall. And this morning, I shall
smile too for those men and women who are my brothers
and sisters knowing the light again.

A Letter From Pt. Hope

"Eat lots of seal oil."
That's what this Inupiaq says.
"For the winter cold bitter.
Eat lots of seal oil."

Just over the prairie ridge,
there are unseen rocks
jutting to the north. There,
right there are the waiting seals.
And underneath the miles, miles
of eternal ice all around,
there are more unseen seals.
"You just have to wait too."

And sing songs very, very softly.

The Right Instinct

Yesterday afternoon, bravely
and foolishly I set out for Mission.
To test the road, test myself.
The wind was direct and fierce.

                              The road
could go anywhere, nowhere.
The ridge was clear, road blown clear,
but going down and westward
suddenly it was a glacial planet
in a deathly white galaxy.

                         Nothing
but the wind and snowdrifts claiming
the road, the nerves of my body

and quickening mind, everything.
It doesn't take much more than a mile
to figure it out.

                My imagination
is a safety net.

                Turn back. The wind
is friendless, even the prairie hills
feel safer hiding. Nothing is certain
but the instinct for safety and survival.
Nothing else to know but to turn back.

It was snowing in the morning and the wind was blowing.
Down here near the creek in a little low valley, it's not so bad,
trees and hills all around. Once I got out to the highway and
turned southwest, the ridge road was mostly clear. But at
the top of the ridge and going down, suddenly the wind was
stronger. And then it grew worse. A snowdrift had plunged
halfway across the road. And then a quarter mile further,
another snowdrift, this one higher, reaching halfway up the
cab of the truck. It could only grow worse. The wind was
pushing beyond itself, blinding everything. I had chasms of
feeling like going into an eternal frozen silence. Nothing but
white and the compelling surge of wind. Finally, without a
sign of where it led, the highway disappeared into a white
darkness. So the intuition-mind takes over any thrust of the
heart. It does not want to leave it any choice, no decision but
the one most needed. Fear is a viable and effective option.
And so I turned back, came home, singing.

That was four days ago. Today, I'm still singing.

The Wind Doesn't Know
What To Do But Be Blue

The wind is blue
this morning
                    so blue, ooooing
at a lonely corner
of the house.

                    Look at the sun.

                                        Look
                    at the sun.

But it pays no mind.
Just so blue, it says,
just sooooooo blooooooooooo
                            looooo
                                        blue.

Blooooooooo ooooo oo ue.

Whatcha gonna do.
I don't know.
Whatcha gonna do.
I don't know.
The blues are blue.
The blues are blue.
The wind is blue.
It goes oooo.
It goes oooo.
Whatcha gonna do.
It goes oooo.
The blues go oooo.
I don't know.
That's what I'll do.
That's what I'll dooooo.

There's a bright prairie sun but the wind just doesn't notice. It
rattles the windows a bit without strength. It's sunny, I keep

saying, telling the wind. It's cold some but it's not bad, but it doesn't listen. Heart, I say, you're not bad either. Tell the wind not to be blue. But it's blue, heart says, it's blue. I know, I say, but it's sunny out though it's cold too. It's cold too, the wind says, cold tooooo. Goes like that at some corner of this house. So I'll leave it be, just write down its blue words, nothing I can do. Nothing I can do, the wind says. Nothing I can do but be blue, that's what I'll do, the wind says. Bright sun, I insist and I know my heart insists too, but the wind, the prairie wind, it's so true it will do nothing but what it wants to do. Be blue, go oooooo ooo oooooo even the sun's gonna get blue.

Never the Moment Until Now

Every day we drive
the road from Mission to Okreek.
It's the same prairie, the same
timeless wind though seasons change
surely, and we change.
But it's the same nevertheless.
It's said as a truism: change
and yet all remains the same.
And so we drove on the same road
from Mission several days ago.
And we looked to the southwest—
there. There within the sameness
were the few trees, barelimbed now,
outlined on the horizon just as
they have always stood. But now
sparkling.
        Sparkling between us
and the low afternoon sun, sparkling.
It's the same horizon, the same few trees,
and the same sun, the same season
of ice, it's true. And now sparkling,
this moment has never been,
and we've never been,

our eyes, hearts, spirits have never been.
This moment of the ice sparkling
on tree limbs can only be now.
We could travel this same eternal road
throughout all creation's time
but this sparkling moment
will never be known until now
nor ever again.

Nothing and Everything

For three nights the moon
has been so bright through the trees.
It felt like something breaking. It seemed
so fragile, the moments no longer possible.

On this night, the fourth, it is not
like that though I've waited for its light.
And now, there is only the glow
not a promise but the always moon.

          The trees
will stand as always, still in winter,
the cold steady forever. Nothing is
that tenuous and only momentary light.

It fades always. It could have been love.
So it was just the moment we caught between
us, nothing but that and everything.

The three nights and one more breaking
our hearts, the moons we've always been.

Moon and the Night

Out with the night,
quietly her moon rides the mountains,
deserts, riverbanks to this prairie in winter.

What for? It's not safe anymore, the matter
has been settled for years; generations
have gone by now in peace and war.
So the quiet night
is now once again its own,
nothing to be on the lookout for.
Let the moon linger at the edge of trees.
We, like moon and trees,
find ourselves wintering, still fragile,
desired as a distant night.

Destination, Seeking

Early this morning, the moon glides
into the galaxy that is my soul.
Everything is huge, dimensions so vast
there is no need to seek significance.
A silver glow tilts the prairie hills
toward the impossibly held balance
we have never easily been able to achieve.
My soul has not been impossible to deceive;
I've plumbed its depths beyond its limits
and found planets wandering like lost children.
I've believed we could find our way home,
but the distances I have carefully mapped
do not reach the destination sought.
This morning's moon has only its significance.
I cannot have the glow of its body for my own.
I only owe myself the humility of seeking it.

JANUARY 28

Looking for Morning Birds

The birds nesting
for the winter
in the garage eaves
tell me morning

is now here. Yes,
I see, I answer
their shrills, aware
of their moments
in this blue light.
I was just thinking
if I were on Uranus
how I would miss
the birds, mornings.
It wouldn't matter
if the sky were full
of moons. I'd look
for the morning sung
presently by the birds.

In the evening several days ago, I went to get the frozen laun-
dry from the line out back. Suddenly, above me in the stand
of pines and spruces, there was a furious flapping. Rapid-
fire beating of wings. A dozen or so pheasants roosting for
the night, disturbed by me. I felt forlorn, having bothered
something, having come upon something that had settled for
the time. I felt like that moment I stopped once just in time,
just as I was about to step on a nest of blue-mottled eggs.
Forlorn, being places I don't belong. How much the human
species is like that, as if it were God's special little joke on the
world created. If I belonged, there would have been no need
for the pheasants to be driven suddenly from their roost, ter-
rified of the possible hunter I was. I didn't do anything, just
stood there before the clothesline, hearing them, watching
them, busy shadows bursting out of the trees in the blue eve-
ning light. When I got the clothes from the line, they were
stiff and unwieldy, cold as ice to my hands. When I looked
again at the pines and spruces, nothing was there but the
prairie evening coming rapidly from beyond.

Out There

The prairie ridge
to the west
across the creek
holds the moon.

From a core
only blood knows,
a howl flies
through the trees.

Dark swaying
motion and tremor.
Welcoming the dark.
Eternity and now.

Outside, the dogs
quiver wildly,
lost in time,
aching for the past.

My own moon twin
cannot be denied.
The wild sway holds
me on the ridge too.

So it happened. It could have been only a story, just a story
with a fictional setting, carefully worded by a gifted writer,
the story drawing the reader completely into its plot, char-
acters, mood, theme, and outcome from the beginning,
through the middle, to the end. Just like any good fiction, just
like any good story. But this time, it happened. It wasn't just
a story. Although years from now, people will wonder: What
was the name of that spaceship? Explorer? Discoverer? Con-
queror? Challenger? And maybe, just maybe, someone will
remember that old man asking, "And then will they know?"

A Savage Dream

The destiny of stars
boils inside the mind.
The thrust of savage intent
cannot be harnessed.
The real dream fades away.
Mankind doesn't learn much
in many thousands of turns
of millennia. He fetes
his hope beyond the dream.
Countless may be killed
but not from <u>his</u> dream.
Only the intended power
can be held to account.
The stars are steady
in their cycles, destiny
is within them, dreams
always as they've been.

So we add only more deaths
to our side, the foolish
rending of our sacredness.
Mankind is with the stars.
The cosmic mirror shines
not from endeavor but praise
when there is the humility
for believing in a real dream.

The scene is shown on television over and over and over
again.

It is silent. It is distance wrought by electronic wizardry. Faces
of American folk shining, joyous, triumphant. Gleaming.
Rockets burst on the ground, flames and smoke push the
vessel upward, the spaceship rising and rising. Into silence. It
could be praise, it could be a blessing, or it could be sacrilege.
Upward. The shining faces turned to the sky. It could be any-
where but there it is on the Florida coast. And then in long,

silent seconds, everything comes apart. It could be a dream. It could be a nightmare. Everything comes apart. Render unto God what is God's. This one belongs to Caesar. White plumes slowly rend apart, shards of the ship plummet in slow motion, it is mad art, the sky doesn't change, and there is only the vast silence.

The televised faces of American folk tremble with excitement for a while, then quaver between joy and tragedy, then break into dismay, then fall into an even deeper silence of the unaccepted, all held within the awesome moment that is Creation and All-Life. Faces—children, their parents, old people, strangers—faces. They are before us in silence, behold them. We are no stranger to loss certainly. It's been our relative forever. And in this moment, it is right here, behold.

Television, the wizardry that is the province of this generation, repeats it over and over and over again.

Keeping Pain and Sorrow

Almost midnight and winter so quiet,
the wind sunk into the prairie lee.
The disturbance is only a subtle pain,
the one that sits so close to the bone
it's almost not there. Yet is there,
a shadow of something, an onerous echo.
We can't turn back time. We know better
it seems, even vainly, and we accept it.

The echoed pain nonetheless bothers me,
not moving except as I move this time
and another. A moment ago, it's there,
and I breathe it away, then it's back.
Sorrow doesn't grow old, it glows dimly
in a cold kind of durable, lasting light.
We feel it cannot really ever go away,
and I think thus: let it always keep,

a throbbing of memory, a precious stone
that is like this hour close to midnight
and the winter so quiet, the wind at lee.

Too Fast at 45 MPH

From here to there
we quiver on loose skin,
the rolling cells washing us
into the storming river.
I think that yesterday,
driving too fast I know
on Highway 18, heading east.
It's frozen mud, snow, ice,
and the flanks of the prairie
are solid, yet tenuous.
How we design our mornings,
as I've done this one,
doesn't matter. It's still
the trick of exact notice
we don't accomplish well.

Forty-five miles per hour
is not too fast, but the edge
is right there. It will not
take much for the atoms
to pull suddenly akimbo,
one disintegration too soon.
My skin is not precious
enough after, and I am mere,
a presence of hope, faith,
too much ego, loose luck.
The quiver I read well
for my sake, hoping for it
to be dependable enough.

Horses by a Fence

Feeding on dry alfalfa.
Woods behind them along the creek.

They were there,
a mare and her colt.
Once in my life,
I've been there.
A moment is enough.
Fog in my mane.
Lightning in my eyes.
Molten lava blood.
Flower petals my soul.
Finally, that once
of a moment is found.
But for that,
nothing is there.

Dawn Prayer for All

Right before dawn, in the blue light of it,
I look for the horses but they aren't there.
Only the winter trees, thick along the creek.
Everything is still, not even birds move. Only
a pain in my chest under my right breast.
Pulling muscle, something engorged, I'm afraid
of its motion, the turn I awaken to daily.
The horses must be beyond the creek, feeding
in the frozen meadow. I'll not wait for them.

My knowledge is only human, only my eyes see
what is to be seen, and beyond that is more
yet it is not within my ken. I can't see death
yet know its presence well, even its posture
prior to it. Pain is not death, I allow that.

For that I am grateful to my mind, the memory
ancient, not lonely or unreasonable. Pray then
for the blue light of morning that draws me
toward the day. Pray then for the horses,
for the presence of all things, for the pain.

Meeting on Stage

Sleek pheasants start crossing the road
before me, before the metal bulk
I'm driving.
They hesitate, then one dares
the distance and velocity,
makes it across.
The other twirls, dancing
at the edge of the asphalt,
the stage.
It takes but an instant
before I reach the spot
of the crossing.
It takes but a second
for it to sink in:
how distance and speed
is none of our control.
We live around it,
the pheasants dance,
my briefest hesitation
before the crossing.
The stage is ready, set.
We never know more than that,
coming to each other there.

As Aliyosho approached a spring, he saw an old horse. The
horse's ribs were showing, and it had sores all over its body.
Terrible-looking running sores, and all around there was the
smell of death. Aliyosho was afraid and he started to turn
away. But he turned back, and he said, "Beloved old horse, I

will bring you some water." The old sick horse had tried to get to the spring, but it had not been able to because it was too weak. Aliyosho brought it water to drink, and then he poured water on it to cool the hot painful sores. The old horse was now able to stand on its feet, and Aliyosho said, "I have to go now as I am on my way to see the king in the south. My mother is very old, and we are poor. I am going to try and win the prize the king has offered. I'll go now." As Aliyosho turned to go, he heard the horse softly say, "Thank you, son, for giving me water. You have helped this old sick horse. You are a compassionate man. I want to help you too. What do you need, young man?"

At first, Aliyosho could not believe the horse was talking to him. He had been walking across the desert for a long time, needing water, and maybe his mind was going strange. And then he said, "I have been walking for a long time now. I'm afraid to be late, because I have to get to the rey's house on a certain day, and I'm in a hurry. I'm sorry but I don't think you can help me." And then the old horse said, "My son, go to the spring, get water again. Bring it and pour it all over me." Aliyosho looked at the open sores again, and even though he was in a hurry he brought some water, and he poured the water over the horse. And as he did so, the sores washed away and in their place were white spots. The old horse became Caballo Pinto.

No, The Story Is This Way

Aliyosho had to get to the rey's house
on a certain day. Otherwise, he'd be too late
for the contests that were going on.
So he said to the sick horse, "Beloved Horse,
I have to be going as I am hurrying."
And he turned to go, and the old horse spoke,
"My son, I know you are in a hurry,
and you've been traveling for a long time.

The rey's house is far from here still,
and you can't be late in getting there.
But can you linger just a while longer?
Before you go, can you again bring water
from the spring and wash my painful sores?
Please." The horse said this quietly, crying.
Aliyosho did not have a minute to spare,
he knew he had to be on his way. But he went
for the water and gently washed the sores.
"Beloved Horse, may you get well," he said
kindly, truly wishing the horse good health.
And as Aliyosho washed the horse, the sores
vanished and in their place were white spots.
The old sick horse became Caballo Pinto
who said, "Thank you, my son, for doing that
for me. You have compassion and love. Now
get on my back for I am a young horse again,
and I'm quite fast enough. I can help you."

Coming To Know

Fog melds the trees,
the frozen ground, this house,
the prairie hills. Everything
becomes one thing, apparent
as such. How much we forget this,
the necessary knowledge
we have to hold
so we can be held.

If I went outside
I would be absorbed
by the prairie universe
of trees along creek banks,
frozen ground, roads,
everything, and become how
it has always been.

I would know again.

Night Horses

Quickly, before my breath knows
what I am doing, their hooves roll
thunderous and treacherous toward me.
Seeing is a sudden strain. My ken
is only a darkening cloud of light.
It is unbidden fright I sense, frantic,
urgent, and unresolved, waiting
for my mind to settle in decision.

This evening I merely went into the backyard
to get this morning's laundry from the line.
And now, the fear unsettled in my stomach
comes rolling out of the dark to my feet.

But they are horses afterall. Yes,
I see them soon clearly enough, this side
of the shadows beyond. Their shapes
emerge into the forms I love, I know,
the nudge of their breaths enclosing
the air we breathe. They are dark within
the greater dark of night at the end
of the line stiff with our frozen clothes.
Yet for a moment I could not fully know
why I was throttled by the sudden motion
of fear, the quickly entering fluid force.
I could only refuse to accept the dark there.

Now, the gentle horses linger at the edge
of the assured moment, and they wait for me.
Our knowledge of fear is vast, and it is
our knowledge of the greater dark of dark.

David calls Tom a cynic because Tom says you can't build a
good house for five thousand dollars. "When I build mine and
it lasts five hundred years, then people can tell me what they
want to," David says. I laugh at the antics of my friends and
what they say.

We do what Charley tells us, and we make joking replies as we help him on Saturday. The long pine beams are heavy, bulky, the ground is slippery with mud and snow, and at moments it's not so funny but we laugh. It's amazing how Charley's done it. Handiwork and more: belief and art: ingenuity and concept, paying careful attention to things. Here he is, Charley, an American white man married to a Lakota woman, and they live here on Lakota land along the Little White River. It is possible to pay attention to land and have a belief, art, and ingenuity. And be a white man married to an Indian woman.

The center beam is the heaviest, fourteen feet long, solid pine, and we grunt, cuss, heave slowly, trying to take care. Anything can happen just like that, too much weight to handle and hold, a sudden slip. Charley tells us firmly, "Plan which way to jump." We laugh. Knowing how and which way is always good advice.

Charley measures another roof beam to fit. We watch as he pencils lines, plugs in the power saw, saws, then chisels. He doesn't listen to Tom's extra advice until Tom has to say, "You're alright, Charley. You're pretty damn good." We heave the beam, struggle with it, but it fits. Just like that, the beam fits.

Afterwards, we sit in the kitchen at their trailer, tell stories, jokes, drink coffee. We know this much: this man and woman's house will last a long time because it was built to be strong as belief, art, ingenuity, concept, and, most of all, prayer and respect, all of that a holy fit.

Joined

"I put sage in every joint,"
Charley says as he prepares the beam.
Puts a sprig of sage in his mouth,
and we—Tom, Harvey, David, and I—

lift and carry the beam to his new house.
Lift it and jiggle it until it fits
on top of the outer wall
and the center post, and Charley,
with his first finger and thumb,
carefully puts moist sage into the joint.
There. It fits now, the people, land,
the sacredness, sky, and walls joined.

Ordinary Moments

Jim Bob is already out this hour
of the morning by his barns.
It's not so early though, sun is above the horizon.
A February morning. Yesterday's fog is gone.

"Maybe there'll be an early spring,"
he said the other day, standing by his truck.
Ground's been thawing some, mud's everywhere.
"You oughta be over here," he said, lifting a foot.
His boots are more than ankle-deep in prairie gumbo.
I mentioned the horses, noted their skinnyness.
"They get like that in the winter," he said.
"You oughta see my riding horses. They're worse."

Later I was out back. Jim Bob called me over
and asked what size tires I put on my truck.
He showed me a tire in the back of his truck.
"I used to have a Dodge like yours and I got these.
Found them just now again and I said to myself
you just might have use for them.
I got three more, same size as this," he said.
I asked him how much he wanted for them.
They're too much, I don't really need them,
not right now anyway. I said I'd let him know.

We're neighbors and our work is different,
and we talk like this sometimes. Ordinary talk,
weather, gumbo, horses, winter, trucks, today.

The Prayer-Rain Is Here

Tuesday rain, morning, and blue light.
I could hear it, waking up, sound
of water pouring quietly off the roof,
down the gutter pipe
                    to the ground.
Under this house below prairie grass roots,
the earth gathers up the rain, regenerates it
in huge caves, lovingly moves it about
within the cycles of the planets and suns.

It's this we perceive at the edge
of this rainy dawn, the water trembling
and gentling off the roof. It's this prayer
which insists we notice and cannot avoid.
It's Tuesday morning rain right now.
It could be California, Pacific Ocean clouds
like horses flying over coastal hills,
across desert valleys, over the mountains
toward the Lakota prairie.
                    It could be,
but, right now, it's here, a Lakota prayer-rain.

Loss and Grief Finding Us

On the death of a young poet

Yesterday, the slightest tremor
could have avalanched even the prairie.
Everything was tenuous, edged at a precipice.
Everything leaned toward loss.
It was grief which stalked us, found
us days later and too soon, too soon.
Winter's freezing rain and icy roads
were vengeful it seemed to us yesterday.

Unjustified. And what could we say?
Friend, sister, poet, warrior, human.
When grief finds us, we learn of loss.

It is this knowledge of mortal life
and irredeemable error which finds us grieving
and sensing too much loss.
                              We know better
than to be found stolen away in shadows.
But it's true too, we'll be found, from time
to inevitable time, to be parents of a lost child
who will remind us of the ancient tremor.

This morning the ice is as steady as the earth
has always been in winter, and a mist veils
the Lakota prairie hills. Loss and loss will stalk us,
finding us too soon and there could be the tremor
across everything. But we will hold and hold.

Three. On Tuesday, Halmi and I were suddenly halted in our conversation in the parking lot on campus. We stared at each other, our eyes holding for several seconds or more. Gunfire. Two rifle shots, then after a brief pause, a third ringing through the frigid air. The ringing hangs, having shattered the prairie quiet.

Later. I learn it was a funeral, a Lakota military veteran honored by gunfire cracking the winter air, bullets whipping silence away. For him, a rest beyond this life. For us, knowledge that death is common enough, manageable as a concern, and a familiar destiny.

Later. Her death is vastly troubling. It is more shocking since we don't know anything about timeliness. She was gifted, a human spirit glad and grateful for herself. Yet troubled, unable to forgive injury done her spirit. Nothing soothes this more than death itself, a shadowed mirror before us. Still, it rankles us that we feel our rational and bearable humanity is a common error.

Later. From out of a darker region, the evening news is brought to us starkly of a sixty-seven-year-old farmer who brought his life to the doorsteps of justice in a South Dakota town. This time he determined the judgment, not the judge nor God. It was simple enough to pull the trigger in broad daylight, law and God standing by.

These were only three.

In My Life

Wake up to cold weight invisible
in the house. There. Gas ran out
sometime during the night, again.
Don't put on water for coffee, no use.
Take a lukewarm shower, wash hair.
Mornings in my life, like these.

A friend and I were talking yesterday afternoon about a recent meeting on the newest law from Congress. Money cutback. Indian people faced with decisions that should never be made. Education decreased simply due to lack of money. My friend had been at the meeting.

"Was there a feeling of anger? Despair? Or was it clear what people were willing to talk about?"

He said, "It was mixed. Some were real angry. Others? Well, accepting, willing to wait some more."

Despair or anger? It's an unfair question. I know what the people feel. Helplessness.

"The federal government is taking advantage of people's down-ness. It knows people aren't in any shape to fight back. Kicking them when they're down!"

He said, "I worked in Los Angeles for six months one time.
Dry walling with Blacks and Mexicans mostly. I was the only
Indian. It wasn't much of a job, just something to exist by.
Existing. Everybody was in that shape. And they told me,
those guys I worked with, 'We're ready to pick up guns any-
time you want us to. Anytime. We're ready. Just tell us when
you people are ready. We'll do it.' And they were, those
Blacks, Mexicans, poor people, they were ready."

Anger? Despair?

"You know, I don't know when we'll be really ready. I mean
we're ready now, but I mean when will we really get so frus-
trated, angry, hurt from being abused. Hungry, tired, insulted,
kept down. Someone, something will start it at just the right
time. The right issue to take action on. Then it'll happen. I
know others are ready."

When Is It Enough?

The gas goes off.
We're cold.
It costs too much.
We're cold.
We have to pay.
For everything.
We're cold.
It hurts.
We work every day.
The gas goes off.
We're cold.
What has to happen?
When it is enough . . .
will it happen?

Near

and

Evident

Signs

of

Spring

He looked toward the frozen creek. Along the creekbank, there were only the gray trees barelimbed. Winter was two months gone by. Where are the rabbits? he wondered. Hares? Jack rabbits? He wondered what the difference was. He didn't know except that jack rabbits were large. Somewhere in the frozen ground, burrows dug before the hard cold came for days, weeks, months back in late November. On a couple occasions, he'd seen tracks in the frozen snow. It seemed to him there should have been more. But there weren't, and he hadn't really looked much for them. It was too cold to be walking around on the windy prairie, looking for rabbit tracks. The gray trees along the creek bottom were always there though. He didn't have to look to know they were. It was like that with the rabbits, hares, jack rabbits, he thought. They were there somewhere in the winter all around.

We and the Light

It changes just like that. One moment the sun
glistening off the snow, winter light quicker
than the eye to connect the sky with all things,

and then without any noticed motion, no turn
of the head, it washes into gray: trees
withdraw their shadows, fence posts blend
into somewhere, the eye is no longer awed.

Everything is a perceived fleeting motion afterall.
Light is relative to dark, the moment is neither
now nor then. We wait, spirit, mind, blood, nerves,
for the image that will catch us again moments away.

When Aliyosho and Caballo Pinto approached the Rey's pueblo, they saw it was a beautiful town lying in a little green valley through which a gentle river flowed. Aliyosho was happy he was finally there, at the end of his journey and on

95

time for the contests where a big prize was offered. And it was because of Caballo Pinto that this was possible. Aliyosho had much to be thankful for, and he said, "Beloved Caballo Pinto, you have been so helpful to me, and so faithful with your supportive spirit, and I could never repay you for your help." Caballo Pinto felt the boy's gratitude, respect, and love in the words he spoke. Caballo Pinto said, "That is alright. Just remember to always be kind and be humble, and you will be successful in your endeavors." And Aliyosho and Caballo Pinto trotted toward the Rey's beautiful pueblo in the valley.

Winter Morning and Me

Only the light doubles itself—
two panes of glass—winter and me—
this morning and waiting for light—
darkness is quietness—at this hour
it's so—momentary and yet eternal—
our own history is beyond us always—
though we're not about to let it—
be, just be, I've been told—yeah,
and it's true—the single light
in front of me on the table doubles
itself on the glass panes—I said.

Television news this early morning is about the Philippines and South Africa. Ferdinand Marcos and Nelson Mandela. How ironic is the spare knowledge we're provided about ourselves. We've come to know so much via the so-called wonder of modern technology, yet we still don't know. The human species jails freedom and encourages the most powerfully corrupt. Dictator and freedom fighter. The irony doesn't end. It's in the knowledge itself the fault lies. Freedom is killed, and the killers are alive.

Stellar Tendrils

The roots still hold us.
The stars still hold us.
South Africa is right here.
South Dakota is right there.
Beneath the people's feet
the roots twine.
Above the people's heads
the stars shine.
Moments become years, time
connects our common life.
It's all one yearning.
Births become generations, children
bond us together.
It's all one knowledge.
The unseen tendrils of light
of stars above us,
the unseen tendrils of dark
of roots beneath us,
they are with us,
for us, and we must hold.

Stories, Words Finding Their Way

Today, here within the moment of this day,
is the tug, the hunger I've held back.
The stories. The words in the stories.
One time it was . . . words . . . then others.
They go on in some way, leading away
from a start, even away from me, and then
finding their own road, getting lost
at times until they discover the way
there is to go. That's the story, words
finding themselves, discovering each other,
always seeking the necessary vision
they must have . . . and then back again,
better off this time, ending and beginning.

Hungry Questions

What does the cosmos
have to do with money?
I don't know.
Within it, we are
moneyless.
Yet, the urgent civilization
we are driven by
is hungry,
not for the knowledge
given by the stars,
not for the succor
of the natural gods.
The tremendous cavity
in the modern gut
is for money.
And we answer the question
with the question,
"What does money
have to do with the cosmos?"
And arrive at no answer,
still hungry.

Keeping Intact

Driving from Mission into the crying blizzarding wind
and snow this evening, I felt
the shift of the continent, its sudden drift
inward, perhaps a relocating of bones and ridges.
There was no thought,
                        no temptation of flying loose.
We are bound to know from time to time
it is possible to lose hold but not right now.
Right now, simply, the tough dry husk of living
shelters us, keeps us intact.

Amazement

Sudden shift in the weather
amazes me, like yesterday afternoon
going to Rosebud it was cold gray,
ice and iron frigidity, day
to not walk into, no sun—
and then not much later,
I step outside into sunlight
so bright and welcoming,
my belief suspended, ice and iron gone.

That's the sudden

                  ness that amazes.

He watched yellow sunbeams blooming on the kitchen wall
and slanting through curtains in the large living room win-
dow. The prairie sun to the east beyond the hills. He was
amazed, amazed like a prayer. It is prayer, he thought, to be
amazed. To be thoughtful as well as prayerful. To praise and
think, a friend said several days ago. He didn't know the intel-
lectual construct of seeing the sun nor the physics of light.
Optics, he thought it was called although he wasn't sure of
the correct term. But he did know he felt praise and thought-
ful. And grateful just for being alive. Other mornings, other
places, he'd been barely alive, simply and ingloriously dying,
sick and hopeless, but now at this moment, watching yellow
light blooming on the wall he was praising. The friend had
used the thought in an essay he'd written and when he men-
tioned it he said it was from Heidegger or Buber or somebody
but it didn't matter. Watching the sunlight on the kitchen
wall, it was praising he felt, simple as prayer, deep as prayer,
a prayer blooming in his spirit.

Night Winter

Right before we go to bed last night,
the cold comes. The fire is not enough,
no matter how much wood, how good the draft,
it would still be cold.

                    The wind curls
into the easiest passage. If none anywhere,
it goes around and bit by bit everything
is deeply chilled. Here, the prairie knows
what must be done, what has to be its soul,
a presence of wind, the surge and flying
away.

                    It is this motion, a wonderful
agility, we can be envious of but are not.
Wakan Tanka, Tunkashila, prays with us
then. The prairie and the winter wind
at night are fearless, each unto itself
and with one another in strong, vital life.

Good Morning, Sun. Thank you, and Good Morning, My Life!

Magic Always

Red fire on the grate,
magic idea,
the cosmos and cell
enjoined,
perfection not sought
but there.
Within the glow and spark,
stars linger
momentary and eternal.
We can only look, pray
the notion
that we're with them,
part of their world.

We're not deer though,
dark woods around us.
We're only human,
fervent and eager,
tricks for magic
in our fingers.
And the red fire's
on the grate, magic
as it always is,
and we're alive
with cosmos and cell.

FEBRUARY 14

More Real Magic

Sunlit pine
snow falls
from a branch
one motion one time
magic one time

Soundless
one time falling
snow one time
for me is magic

Could not have
looked in time
to see it
magic real is that

Light touches
me snow pine
motion and magic
together in time

Prairie sun
and snow touch
reality more
than this moment

Single pine branch
won't break
one time ever
always bend always

Not alone but one
all things in one
snow pine light one
me motion magic one

Buffalo Light Now

Without knowing at first what it is,
I can feel there are buffalo about—
one, two, a great herd, many.
The spirit of Muushaitrah,
more than spirit, this I know.
The horizon of the prairie hills
within us, the spirit within us.
A great shadow of winter hovers,
has for weeks, months,
and this morning right now,
there is no sun but only the light.
It is Muushaitrah though, the song
of its spirit, the Sun:

> Muushaitrah,
> weh dzuutroh,
> weh truhpoh,
> weh tchiahtsastih.
> Dawaa-eh, Aneh eh
> meh-yuunah shrah,
> meh yuunah niieshruu.
> Staidzee, niieshru.
> Staidzee, niieghu.
>
> Da-ah emih, Oshratrah
> Kqaihyuh, Kqooyoutih tah.
> Muushaitrah, dzih-yuutih-tahnih.
> Muushaitrah, stihyuutih-tahnih.

It is this song, this song of light
that I sing for Buffalo right now,
fearfully, lovingly, humbly.
Listen to my song, Buffalo, hear me.
I am only an Acoma man.
Dyaahmih Hanoh shtuudehshih,
Kquutsiwahshtih shtuudehshih,
this yuuni stuuyootitah:

> Buffalo,
> you have come to us,
> you have come in,
> you come about and around.
> Thank you, it is beautiful,
> you are still alive,
> you will always live.
> In everything, living.
> Everything will live.
>
> This is the way, Sun,
> its Song, Singing it is.
> Buffalo, it is singing for it.
> Buffalo, I am singing for it.

As we ride toward Mission and are five miles east of the small
town, we see Coyote. In all that prairie vastness, everything
frozen and blanketed with snow, there it is, crossing High-
way 18. Right before us, everything full of distance. We look
at each other, unbelieving at first, and then back to Coyote
crossing the road. Right there in front us, heading north. It
is real and actual, the truth of Existence within the strangely
beautiful vastness of this prairie. We know we are alive.

Lightyears and the Prairie

Somewhere and some time
beyond star reach
still stands
        a moment caught
within fragment
of shadow . . .

fingers' tip and grasp

Tight solitude at last
stands still
        a second caught
drumming . . .

Something is held within
light

These eons and vastness make sense.
Lightyears and prairie cosmos know.

Box elders are strange insects, seeming lost and without purpose as they wander. Since before the first snow, they've been around everywhere. Of course, they're not lost, they wander here and there, mapping journeys as they make them, as they find them. Perhaps not really sure at moments, but going ahead anyway. It is winter they face, just like we do, but they don't worry much about it. Outside, it's cold but it doesn't make much difference to them. They stay outside, careful about wandering on just the edge of shadow and the margins of light. Odd bits of life, orange filaments burnishing them, their wings extended some as if for ready flight which they seldom perform. Their mystery is mine, since I identify with their wanderings. I'm tempted to follow the box elders, to linger just behind them in their slow trails.

I need them now I think as I watch them skirt corners and edges that could suddenly lose them. They are with seeming unfound purpose, like the psyche that knows a motive but doesn't quite put it to action and words. It's imagination likely that box elders seek and having found it they don't know what it's to do for them. Perhaps I'm wrong, and they know exactly what they're doing. However, box elders signal some kind of threat to be aware of, and they never rest, always fervent with seeking destiny, always urgent to keep on their journey. I thank them, their awareness and endurance. Even while they do not know my imagination, our margins are shared. That's where we live, and there is hope in that because in those margins nothing is strange or odd or lost or without purpose.

The Promise We Live By

On the West Coast, days of rainstorm wrestle
the Coast Range, their wet fury driven landward.
We never quite know what the sky promises,
and there is certain assurance in that fate.
It is for that we wait. We've already weathered
more than promises. They've passed us by.
So I'm not sure this morning when I step outside,
and suddenly it's not winter anymore but some
warm mask that molds the contours of my face
with unbidden warmth. It's almost unnatural
but I hope not, having already found reliable
the promise of loss. My expectation is unfulfilled.

Somewhere within the universe of the prairie hills
is a climate that is yet unnoticed, and from it
is welling a warm rupture of another sure season.
Believe it is not unusual, I urge myself
whose myths are always changing in the light.
So it's this we arrive into daily, always
another season, warm or frigid, and it's we
who wage weather within our furious spirits.

Tomorrow's dawn is a promise that will fulfill.
Never mind if the sky does not quite agree.

Time and Place in Song

From yesterday
the luminescent forms of buffalo
remain with me,
more than memory, more than remembrance.
It is song
and the place of song.
It is time
and the song of place.

That is for the blood on the horizon
of recall,
not history which is insanity
for "civilized men." No,
we should not permit it to be so.

From yesterday
the buffalo forms luminesce
as they always have.
They are memory and remembrance
remaining always
as song in the place
as song in the time
that is not blood of history.

The Sound, Yours

Deeper than echo
despite vacuum and cold,
a sound heaves
from the floorboards.
Urgent and bold, it's a sound
that sways and fills
moments and motion.
Its origin is unknown,
perhaps in solitude, perhaps
in the search for lost things.
The cold within this house
is a burden in the morning.

It waits, savoring time, waiting
for hope it has known before.
I couldn't shiver,
not daring to, though my body
aches for relief.
We have known hunger,
need for shelter, painful days,
and we have known fear
for so long we yearn
for the heaving groan heard
and felt by bone now.
We cannot know loneliness
anymore, the lost solitude,
so we welcome the echo
back to ourselves.

Listen, the sound is soft.
It is borne by you.

Gently Now, the Blue Dawn

Gently now, the keepsake that is night
draws back to silver dark.
                              Gently,
indiscernible and not conscious of motion,
it leaves into blue shade.

I do not know.
I have never known.
I may never know.
But gently, there is this morning changing,
and but for that, a gradual reckoning,
I would not have the night for memory
nor the morning to be my dawn.

Gently now, gently now, gently now, gently
now, the blue changing dawn light comes.

The Margins Where We Live

Overnight, the air froze.
Crystallized. Now, a thin breath
lies on the prairie hills.
Light becomes certain in cold,
not glazing, not luminous,
only captured and stilled.
The margin of reality
is the margin of illusion.
In that margin between
the prairie and us lies space,
vastness that confirms existence.
It's the air frozen
and it's our awareness.
Nothing more, nothing less
confirms our belief.

The road will be deadly
and will still take icy skill
to drive on.
We will have safe passage.
The margins will always be the space
where we live.

Beyond the Margin

Longing goes as far
as the frozen creek stranded
behind the trees.

It's frigid as that.
Nothing can levitate
without hope and relief.

The frozen creek
and the trees are the margin.

The blue light becomes
more than longing.

Beyond that
is our destiny.

I haven't seen him for years, maybe seven. He still has that
direct, unlimited, fierce stare, almost a wild look. An intense
concentration, a focus on your eyes so you can't and don't
want to hold his gaze for very long. His words comical too at
the same time, that is, he finds something humorous in you,
that you all can laugh about. Because it's something you and
he and everyone else identify with. And still an honest and
subjective seriousness. Beyond this even, he is totally honest,
totally subjective, and totally serious. I've never wanted to
be around medicine women and men for too long, although
my grandfather was one. They have something intrinsically
and deeply to do with your life. They do. They enter your
awareness-consciousness when you least expect it, so that
suddenly within that space which has become palpable you're
asked to do something you're not ready to do. Actually, it's
a choice you're given, to be honest and open and aware. Or
not to be. I find myself looking forward to that when I meet
such people, because I need such a choice.

Creating Language

To use language,
the speaker has to know
its real bones, guts, blood,
spirit, mind, heart.
He has to know its pain
and its joy.
He has to know its creation.
And the only way he can

is to know
he is being created
as he speaks it.
He is a creator then
of that language.

This or This

Telling the story, Wahpepah says,
" 'We need unity,' Leonard said.
'Peace and brotherhood.
We need you and you need us.
Together we have the spirit.'

And then he has the Pipe
in his hands, he smokes it,
prays to above, prays to below,
prays all around.

And then Leonard said, 'This.'
                              Holding the Pipe aloft,
looking at all of us,
Indian and White,
and then he turns it around
and over, and puts it
to his shoulder, and sights
along it, and aims it.

And then he said, 'Or this.' "

FEBRUARY 21

Lingering in the Grip

Death doesn't have much of a grip
on life I believe as I drive headlong
into clouds of fiercely driven snow.
Nothing but white blindness,
nothing but motion gripping you
and there is no clear sense of things.

It is blindness that is power
since there is little or no control.
It's lost within that uncontrolled grip.
The urge for life is met blindly
by the urge for death, and there is
no reason left nor much at the end.
It could be that easy to slide
toward death even when faced with it
finally, since how we know ourselves
has to do with an awareness of it.
Not knowing it anymore, powerless
in its blind eye, there is no sense
to it, and it would simply be fateful
without so much as symbol to save us.

In those few seconds it takes to cross
the blind white eye, our held breath
is gathered so tightly, certainly,
we cannot know its release until
we accept it could be lost forever.
It's not, of course. Our urgent selves
have too much concern for burning ego
that keeps us in mind within this world.
It opens up from within the blindness.
It opens to light when dark
would serve us better, a contradiction
that is reliable when nothing else is.
In this entering out of the edge
and margin where we have always borne
full weight all the nuances and notes
of life, we don't really know where
we are nor why or how we have managed
anything so far. Death has not weighed
us yet and found a worthwhile value in us.
No, it has been caught itself blindly,
not noticing that we have not felt fear
at all but simply an old temptation
to linger eternally within the blind eye
of this grip of winter heart and spirit.

Pray First Then

Dawn, oopuh, oopuh.
Dawaah eh, Ahmoo uh. Ahmoo uh.
Sit in my House,
my heart, Dawn.
Thank you, Beloved. Beloved.
Dawn, enter, enter.

My fingers motion thus.
My hands motion thus.
My breath motions thus.
My heart motions thus.
With motion thus, prayer.

Underneath all this February snow, the prairie hills urge tiny root tendrils to be miracles. Miracle, spring is that. Spring is a miracle. Spring is miraculous.

She used the word, "miraculous," in a story. It was in a rather bland sentence but it stood for everything he had ever felt, that he had ever known about Spring. "The beginning of Spring was miraculous," she wrote. Indeed, yes, he thought. The story went on about a little lost girl and a big husky named what—Buck, Bill, Ben, Big? It could have been a big turtle or big goat, he didn't remember. The important thing was that Spring was miraculous. "I like it," he said about her story, but he really meant only the single sentence, in fact only the word.

He didn't care for most of the story although he went over it with her and the rest of the class. He didn't even discuss the sentence much. When he checked around the class, the students were into the story about the lost child and the dog and how the dog saved her and therefore the family and everything. It was a decent story, but he wanted to dwell on Spring being a miracle. He needed a miracle right now, that's why it was so important to him right then. Lately, there wasn't much he could hope for, but like every year of his growing-up days he was searching for the miraculous. And Spring was always that, at least the beginning of it. Right then, with the bleak landscape surrounding the small cluster of college buildings in the midst of an eternal winter prairie there it was, a single little word like a single little green blade of grass or a tiny flower: miraculous.

One of the other students didn't like it, said it was maudlin, too obvious. Well, so what, what else could it be? He didn't say anything though, although maybe it was maudlin. But he wanted to see that blade of Spring grass right then so badly after months of snow and ice and blizzard, he didn't care if it was maudlin or the sentence bland or merely a story about a kid and a dog. The important thing was the coming Spring he hoped eagerly for, that he was searching for.

Within the Circle Always

Shadows lengthen across the snow.
Snow has been melting all day long.
Sky is almost clear, thin clouds only.
The blue sky, the blue sky all around.

The great circle of this earth.
We are within, sometimes with song.
Sometimes the song is not possible.
Nevertheless, we are within, within.

Split kindling out on the back porch.
Deliberate, calculated movements.
How easy these things should always be.
Just heft the tool, spot the right grain.

The winter sun so warm on my back.
How easy all things should be like that.
The blue sky, within the circle of day.
Without the song even, we are within.

After the Storm

In California, lost children wander
around in the aftermath
of storms and floods. Their parents
swept into a huge
and lunging hunger they didn't seek.
Where can hope look
for safe haven?

                    Where can the children
go, the storm raging all around?

There between the stars,
a soft gentle fire in the cold sky—
this is the destiny, finally,
children face, finally.
The mirror deep in front of them,
facing their new history and ours.

In California, lost parents wander
around in the aftermath, a huge hunger
yearning around them, raging still.

FEBRUARY 22

Winter Changing

Beyond the window glass, only the dark
a refracted night. Shadows featureless,
unknown at best and, drawing the curtain,
I can't fathom what it is that I search for.
Winter is withdrawing, the beautiful dragon
sinuous and coldly strong, lunging for months
across the prairie hills is leaving.

                        It is
this night I look for, the shimmering silver
luminescence the moon has been, the hills
one motion and the vale of stars more than ever
the only sinew we have to hold us.

> It may
> yet be possible the stormy cold will writhe
> and fly as the winter dragon has always done.
> And beyond this window, the night moves
> in a dark wonder and awe of the spirit.

Winter is over, I can feel it, and I feel a sadness for its going. It has been days now, not many yet, the weather has been changing. Days growing longer by minutes, not much but enough to tell the sky is different at dawn and at dusk. Something hard and edged and brittle is gone. The prairie grass is worn and withered weary, but the frozen ground is thawing. This winter has been harder than others I've heard some Lakota friends say. Only the very old know and the very young I think. Their experience is receptive to the power of nature, the requirement to make no comparisons anymore or yet. But why I'm saddened by its leaving, I don't know. Perhaps the power I expected to come forth from being in a difficult winter has not shown itself. That's my fault though. Nature is its own and has its own power and existence. Humankind has survived more than changes in climate. Like other creatures of this earth, we've expected that our tenure yields to the force of a creation we cannot replicate. So perhaps I will know it yet, forever caught within its hold, one with the natural sinew and motion of wind, sun, blizzard, rain, sudden squall, new plant and animal life. All signs of my own natural wonder. Winter will end in a few weeks. Although it may snow again, it will not become ever the final one. It only changes as we change. It only becomes one more winter within the cycle of all time. And I am only a man joined with winter turning toward spring.

"Out There"

> Morning is memorized just once
> by a coyote's howl somewhere beyond the trees.
> It's more than dream we've entered,

coming awake. It's the dawn leaving night.
Sometimes it's possible not to hold anything,
and forever is not a real idea. Memory
is what we seek and find in the howl.

A Near and Evident Sign

It could be a signal,
near and evident
of winter's end.
Borne on the silent still cold,
a sound older always
than all the winters we've known.

Returned once again,
nesting somewhere upcreek,
the sign of ending-beginning.
Owl's motion
into the space that closes
upon us, gathering it
and the message we yearn for.

Be it then, nothing more
than that, a moment
entering easily into us.
The signal we receive,
welcoming its return.

Once, it must have been in the summer of 1971 in Colorado,
the owl came, its deep and hollow sound moving into my
terrified heart. It was a summer I was a fugitive and an exile,
trying to save the life I had left. The sound could not have
been anything other than fear. I was at the end of things.
Now, years later at the end of February, I thank the life I
saved. Redemption is possible, we believe. It could not be
anything else we would strive for. The necessary hope cored
within the owl's song is still fervent, and I receive it gratefully,
having come gladly to know my continuance.

Prairie Night Song

The song could be the slope of a hill,
the prairie slant toward the center.
It could be the flute carved of sacred wood,
the song a history of exile and sorrow.
Yes, the night which is quiet and gentle
now that winter is almost over is a song
of ancient return, a gathering of power
that is holy and circled and eventual
as our dream within all creation has ever been.
The song of this night prairie curls softly,
deeply into a welcoming core of the spirit.

FEBRUARY 23

Tomorrow Across the Prairie

Tomorrow across the prairie,
the wind will journey
as it always has.
                    Only we'll drive
like latecomers do, the ones
who don't know
how it is the prairie
shifts.
                    It's always a wonder how
our journeys are achieved, miles
and miles of travel, knowing
one stop will only start
another distance.
                    The prairie
is silent, accepting.
It has had its share of those
who thought they were headed
somewhere.
                    But it knows
they will pause, suddenly aware
of some motion, some noise,

an origin in the mystique
of the pause itself.

                    It's here
our journey will be known,
across this vast expanse
that is the journey of the stars,
the cosmic marks of far hills,
a point of desolation that sorrows.

Having found our way to that pause,
we'll halt only briefly, then lose
ourselves again to the destiny
searching for the spirit tracks
of buffalo arriving on the dawn.

It's the way it is, he thought. Getting up that morning, he
had felt something moving just over his shoulder, just out-
side at the edge of the window. But when he went to look,
even adjusting his glasses on his nose, he couldn't see any-
thing. Nothing was there. And then he went outside, stood
on the porch, looked toward the trees at the edge of the
backyard. Nothing. Just the barns the rancher had and the
rancher's cows which were about to begin giving birth. And
he wondered if somehow that had to do with what he felt
he'd seen.

Buffalo, that's what he thought he had felt. Suddenly just
that, a memory of a life before the present. He looked toward
the steel barns, and there were only the black cows on the
slope of the hill behind the barns. They were not buffalo in
any way, they were just docile, tamed, domestic ranch cows.
But the feeling persisted, and he could not push it away ex-
cept with the final feeling of that is the way it is, the way it's
supposed to be. The feeling of a buffalo dawn had visited
him, and that is the way it really is sometimes.

Prairie Changing Prayer

The small animals across the prairie must wait too.
The blue light changing. Night hunts ceasing.
Uncoiling, nerves set into a separate dimension.

Dawn is to be a prayer, the moments tilted into vow.
For the sacred bond, like a strong staff passed on.
One day is not always the next, but another time.

One moment must contain the first, the initial one.
When it began with the tiniest cell of light, once,
a sound, then the blue light began forever to bloom.

It's the animals that know and the smallest creature.
The one that lives inside of us, margin and the core.
It is this one that passes across the prairie alive.

In the wake of one fading moment, another does rise.
A further night can only become day, the sun's cycle.
Within the remnant of dream, there is always another.

In this blue light then, dawn is a quiet margin, place
and time and event gathered into the sphere of the eye.
Waiting to cross this prairie, the prayer linking all.

For now, the turn of one time into another is nothing.
It is the prairie of blue light that is the dawn prayer.
Only that, the animals and the core in the margin.

One Scar I Feel More

                    Scars.
                    Hair turning white.
I don't usually do it
with any final sense of doing it,
looking for something
and finding it.

I look in the mirror this morning.
There, the scars
and the whitening hair.
Thursday, Friday,
Saturday, Sunday, Monday,
today, days go just like that.
And before we know it,
we have to look.
There we are.

One scar, more
than any other, I feel
more than see.
But it's right before my eyes,
and as I move
my thumb, it pulls
with an uneasy tension,
strong, oddly vibrant.
Pulling against the grain
of easier and natural movement.

It's the scar
of unnecessary solitude,
the wrong ache, giving in
to uncalled passion. It's the one
that's berserk, unfaithful,
resentful, jealous. It's the one
that misses what's better lost.
Now within its thumb,
this appendage of scar
and hindered thrust
waits for me to notice
the latent motion
that will go wrong.

Arc of Light

I dress in front of the dawn.
Naked in the quiet light, my skin
is cold, and I shiver. My eyes
hungry. The act of rising is habit
but I think it must not be. Coming
light is a gathering of all things
into an arc that burns the ice
on the prairie horizon. Ice vanishes.
There is no such dimension anymore
between far and close. Fire consumes.
I cannot touch it with human eyes.
I can only dress myself, poor clothes.
The winter ice turns platinum,
becomes the growing arc, burning.
My eyes are only solace, an excuse,
and they cannot bear the light.
My very nakedness is shown to me.
The ancestor in me urges me to pray.

So it's the burning arc that grows,
transforms the horizon into light.
It's this I must know not as habit
but act and experience, the dimension
of the horizon that gathers things,
my dressing, all things, me, into light.

Rivers and Winter Knowing

Yesterday, coming from the north,
we cross the Cheyenne River
and the White River.
They are full with broken ice,
treacherous jagged pieces
that slow down the rivers.
A sure sign of winter's end.

It's almost too early, something
in the body resists that change.
But it's the rivers that know.
The snow that melts, trickles
into little streams, gathers
into larger ones, then finally
into the Cheyenne and the White.
These seasons have always changed.
Before the glaciers, ferns grew
in warm, moist, lush climates,
and now the winter past is past.
We resist but we know the changing.
The rivers know and winter knows.

MARCH 3

Mirror

We have to expect it will change.
It's never quite clear. We expect it will stay.
Temperate and clear more or less.
But the stars insist on distinct nuance.
Their own source of power reaches for them,
and it is greater than they.
                              And we
are only the tiniest mirror of them, locked
in the precious balance of Creation we share,
locked to them as cells and atoms are to us.
When they fly suddenly askew, even vanish
in a wink, we hurtle away as unheard echoes
into the eternal changing that is changeless.

MARCH 5

Too Late

Late, late night.
Wait for sounds, messages,
anything.

                    Earlier,
dogs howled, something
so far and beyond
yet immediate.
But now nothing.
Simply the unknown moon,
a yardlight, stillness,
and quiet madness.

We drive ferociously
toward nowhere.
Our weariness honed
until everything is critical,
explosions bound
to be uncontained.
We fear the waiting
for sounds that will come.
Nothing can deter this night.
Nothing almost can save us.

Knowing Shadow and Light

An old friend
long unheard from
writes from the west.
Good to be back in touch.

El Paso, Santa Fe,
Colorado Springs, Tsaile.
What these years,
these roads have been
we don't quite know.

What did she look like?
What did you look like?
What did she write?
What did you write?
There are reasons
for the questions

and reasons for answers.
But right now
the knowledge of the past
is a shadow and the light
is the sun of those years
back then, and it's said
the galaxy shifts
every once in a while.

It does, it does,
and we will never quite know.

MARCH 10

Flying

Into the jolt and swirl
of clouds hanging
above earth,
                    we don't mention
anything about death
and fear.
                    Simply hang on
to the silence.

It's not always so.
Death and fear are the throttle
forming us.
The clouds wait for us, their forms
more complete than ours.

There could be more
we strive toward,
a meaning for death and fear,
utter motion
no one else knows.

It's this we fret about
more than anything else.
The jolting and swirling

cannot be lost.
We must know
the surge of our lives.

Three Days Before Spring, Snow Again

It's still snowing.
This time I have to think
it's been since November
and it gets old.

Trees burdened with it,
looking tired
as the back of my neck,
staggered by the cold weight.

Wind is up again,
swirling and pushing around
like it had nowhere to go,
losing and finding things
and losing them again.

It can't go into despair,
I realize that.
We're more than enough
to hold out as usual.

We don't really know though.
It could be we're tough enough
and it doesn't matter
that the cold and wind
will go on forever.
We're stuck for days and days.
Spring doesn't have a chance.

At the Gas & Git

I'm getting gas.
Had just gotten out of the truck,
and I turn for the nozzle,
and I notice the flash.
I thought it was the way
I turned my head,
an odd second of wondering,
trying to retrace my exact motions,
picturing myself,
but I can't remember everything.

And then I hear the rumble
beyond the Gas & Git,
beyond the snow-hazed distance,
rolling and gathering
all that's eventually to come:
                forth and forth, the power
                unraveling its visceral voice,
                my sinews trembling,
                my mind accepting the flash
                I thought was only a turn
                of my head without intention.

Now, I'm sure of the Shiwana returning,
feeling their gently soothing thundersong.
Now, I know of the Shiwana returning,
hearing their gently soothing thundersong.

MARCH 21

Our Eagerness Blooms

In the shadows beyond the creek,
now only patches of snow remain.
Greening growth is soft urgency.
Eagerly, we dug the soil yesterday.
We kept looking at the browning hills.

It doesn't matter if it snows again.
We're fearless as the coming spring.
It could never be the same as last month.
The moving earth tells us that.

The shadows are luminescent, eager
to receive the early spring light.
Trees, we can tell, are growing supple.
Last night, a sensual odor flew
through the window we didn't close.

What sure sign there is comes gradually.
We trust our eagerness is not foolish.
It's not, and although spring may disappoint,
always it is ready to receive us again.
Snow hides into shadow, and we bloom.